Kicking Ace
Taking Names

by

Jeremy Vandekar

The contents of this book regarding the accuracy of events, people, and places depicted; permissions to use all previously published materials; and opinions expressed; are the sole responsibility of the author, who assumes all liability for the contents of this book and indemnifies the publisher against any claims stemming from the publication of this book.

International Standard Book Number 13: 978-1-60452-071-2
International Standard Book Number 10: 1-60452-071-X

Library of Congress Control Number: 2011943285

BluewaterPress LLC
52 Tuscan Way Ste 202-309
Saint Augustine Florida 32092-1850
http://www.bluewaterpress.com

This book may be purchased online at -

          http://bluewaterpress.com/kicking_ace

Dedications:

> **To God**
>
> **To my beautiful wife, Meg**
>
> **To the Marines who fell**
>
> **To the ones left standing**

Contents

ARS Compound

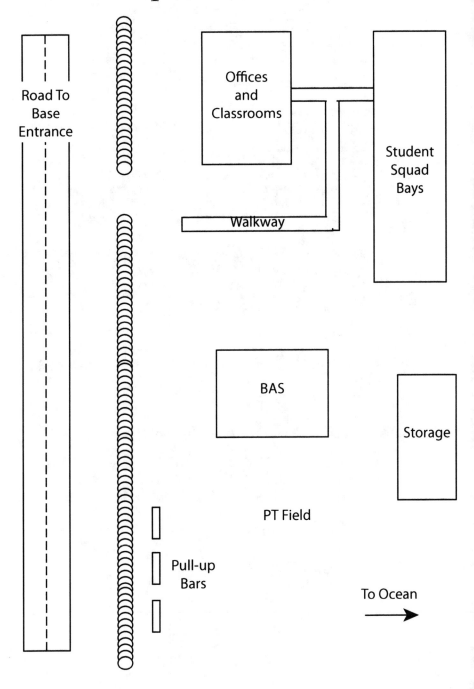

The Point

Y ou may be reading this for a number of reasons, personal or professional. Hell, I'm writing this for a multitude of reasons myself. The idea to write a book all started in Iraq in 2006 when I wrote home to show my family and friends the new experiences I was going through. I wanted to show them the culture, people, food, and military that the media didn't necessarily portray.

The emails became popular and as people forwarded them, my fan club grew. By my second deployment in 2007, I had a large following with people reading my emails in NASA, the Lion's Club, convents, synagogues, real-estate blogs, Washington DC, and around dinner tables.

People said to me, "Write a book! You have all the words – just format it." That seemed like an excellent idea, but there were already plenty of books on Iraq. What made my book any different?

Initially I liked the idea of writing a book, but I didn't find the motivation to begin after I left the USMC and I put it off. "People read my emails because it was happening NOW. They won't read my book because it's already old news," I thought. This excuse was just a reason to be lazy. However, there was a collection of events that enabled me to continue to journal my experiences from Iraq.

When I left the USMC, I started to have trouble adjusting to life outside of Recon: Post-Traumatic Stress Disorder. My social worker told me to write my thoughts and nightmares and then read them to her. It would help to calm me down and collect my memories. When the memories resurfaced again, I wouldn't have such a "startle reaction" to them.

This therapy seemed to make sense but I felt repulsed by the notion that I had PTSD, like I was some crazed lunatic. So I wrote a few stories and stopped. I also found that writing the stories left my mind in Iraq even after I stopped writing. Wasn't the point of this exercise to stop thinking about Iraq?

In another instance, my girlfriend (now wife) was teaching students how to write memoirs and asked me to write down some of my experiences in Iraq. I wrote down two very graphic memories and shared them with her classes. It was one of the first times that I shared some of the more horrific experiences I went through. It was impulsive, but I felt that the students benefited and learned from the information. They weren't offended by the graphic nature of the stories and some thanked me after class for my service. The whole experience helped me to open up and encouraged me to talk to others.

Shortly after the memoirs, my dad's birthday came the same time it always does, in November of 2009. This year, though, he said he didn't want anymore "stuff". My mom also remarked that for her 53rd birthday (2 years away at the time) she wanted my book, nothing else. I began to write down some stories for them without putting too much thought into it and before long, chapters started to form. It was the first official structured "book" that I had attempted and I thought I could get away with cut and pasting my Iraq emails into a Word document.

I took the individual notes and memories from the memoirs, therapy, and stories, and began to put them into a loosely formed book. At first, I had a bunch of incidents that held no congruency. But as more people prompted and encouraged, I slowly began to shape the words into a narrative about my experiences.

What you have before you now is an unfinished memory. I say unfinished because there are things I remembered incompletely or couldn't quite remember completely, if you catch the difference. This book is just an attempt at conveying to you my narrow view of the USMC and the small scope of Iraq I saw.

The title coarsely summarizes the two main skill sets of a Reconnaissance unit: capturing or killing the enemy ("Kicking Ace") and gathering intelligence ("Taking Names"). The Ace of Spades was also used in Vietnam by Recon Marines as a psychological weapon.

The Recon skill-set and Recon history is explained in greater detail later in the book.

I will try to explain everything simply, so if you're an old hand at 782-gear, OSMEAC, blue bodies, or IED ROEs then bear with me as I dissect my brain for the benefit of everyone else. For those of you who haven't served a day in the military, there should be adequate information to keep you up to speed.

Several names have been changed to protect the identity of people involved in the stories.

I don't claim to know all the inner workings of Iraqi culture, nor have I explored every sandy home overseas. I've only deployed twice to Iraq and was stationed in Camp Lejeune during my four years in the active Marine Corps. But what I do know is that more people are in the dark than people who are in the know. The idea for this book is to give the reader a picture of Iraq from the eyes of an enlisted Marine.

Prologue

I looked across from my seat on the C-130, a military aircraft the equivalent of a jet airliner. A 6'8" Marine named Yohe sat opposite me joking about the urgency to pee. He had already deployed to Iraq. My nerves were tight but I joked as well, looking around at the other Marines as we approached Camp Al-Taqqadem, the air base where we would be landing.

We sat on red cargo netting with the ugly paneling of the plane's interior exposed. It looked like someone had started to assemble a plane and stopped halfway through building the insides. We sat straddling our rucks, wearing our Kevlar helmets and flak jackets, and holding our rifles between our legs. My entire company was there, a little less than half of the Iraq-bound 2nd Reconnaissance Battalion crammed with our gear inside this plane. There were close to 60 of us. A Co. would follow in another plane load of Marines. Ahead of us, the advance party from our battalion was already at Camp Fallujah, prepping the offices and equipment for our arrival.

The plane suddenly dipped and banked. There was a loud POFF-POFF-POFF sound from the sides of the plane. "Great," I thought. "I'm two minutes in Iraq and I'm already under attack, helpless inside this bullet magnet." I looked around with a startled expression at the other experienced guys around me.

"Relax, T-Cup," Yohe said to me. "It's flare from the plane to throw off an attack. The turns are evasive maneuvers. All planes do this when they enter Iraq."

As the plane touched down and the ramp lowered, I glanced towards the rear of the aircraft and saw the legendary country for the first time. I had been told I was coming here from day one in the United States Marine Corps. As the heat invaded the aircraft, I could still hear my drill instructor's tyrannical prophecy from Boot Camp:

"LET ME SHIT YOU STRAIGHT KNUCKLEHEADS; 100 PERCENT OF YOU ARE GOING TO IRAQ!"

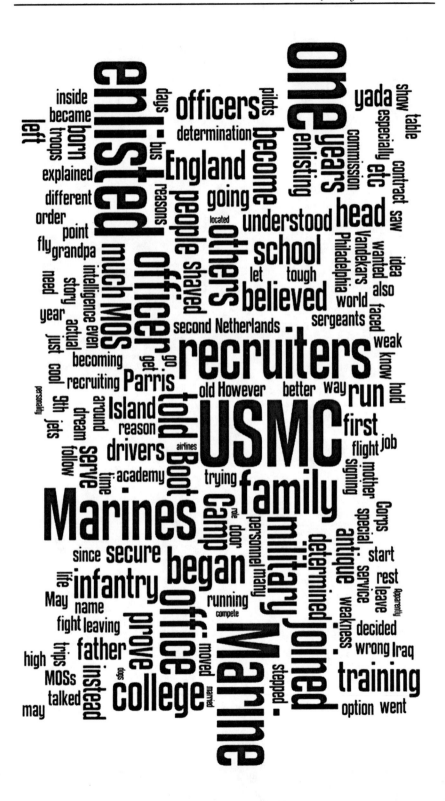

Why I Joined the USMC

"Get the fucking door! What the hell is you're problem?!" the drill instructor yelled at me. I had just stepped off the bus at Parris Island and was the first on the infamous yellow footprints. When he had told us to get inside, I had simply run through the doors leaving the recruits behind me to follow. Now, as a member of a platoon, when we entered a building, one of us would hold the door at the position of attention while the others passed through. Thus began my transition from civilian to Marine.

Ironically, I left for Parris Island, SC on Mother's Day (May 9th) of all days, 2004. I had shaved my head and begun running up and down the hills around my house in Berwyn, PA, a suburb north-west of Philadelphia. For weeks I had been preparing myself physically and mentally for whatever lay ahead. I was determined to pass even if I didn't understand entirely why I was doing it.

Like many Marines I talked to, the reasons why I joined the USMC were many and convoluted. One Marine faced with drug charges had joined instead of going to jail. A few people had heard the call from 9/11 and patriotically joined to fight against our nation's enemies. Some others were at a dead end in life or their family members were Marines. Each Marine told you one story one day and a different story the next. We all stepped into a Marine recruiting office and bought into the adventures they sold us.

The Vandekars originated in the Netherlands. The name van de Kar literally means "of the cart" which is what I presume my straightforward ancestors were doing when they decided to pick a name in the early 1500's. In 1914, when World War I threatened Europe, my great grandfather (being Jewish) fled to England. He was an antique dealer, and England was the center of the art world at the time. The Vandekars who stayed were later killed in the Holocaust.

My grandpa, now born in England, joined the British military, specifically a special enlisted unit called Q Branch. During his service, he was shipped to Iraq in order to fight the pro-Nazi Iraqis and fend off the Russians.

When he returned, he married an Englishwoman and had a son (my father) who became a second generation Englishman. When my grandpa died, my father helped run the antique shop with my uncle and took repeated trips to the Netherlands. On one of these trips, he ran into my mother, a stewardess on KLM airlines.

I was born in England to an English father and a Dutch mother. My dad had inherited his father's antique business and going off of a gut instinct, decided to move to America in order to better serve his clients. Packing up his three kids (all under the age of 8), he moved to the Philadelphia area to begin the American dream. Later, I would follow in my grandpa's footsteps and become the second Vandekar to step in Iraq, though with a different nation.

I had started to show an interest in jets when I was 15 or 16 years old. I went to a few recruiters who told me that I couldn't attend their academies because I was born in the UK. The Navy and Air Force recruiters told me that 90 percent of their pilots come from an ROTC or the academy. I was not a U.S. citizen so both of those options were out for me. I went to the Marine recruiters who explained that the USMC did not have an academy and Marine officers could be guaranteed a flight contract, unlike the other branches that compete for flight slots. Simply put, a non-citizen could become a pilot in the military through the USMC. Sign me up.

The recruiters I had talked to were a part of the enlisted office instead of a commissioned office. The difference in enlisted military personnel and officer personnel is that the officers utilize their college degree to secure a commission whereas the enlisted sign a contract to serve a specific period of time (2 years, 4 years, etc.). The officers serve a supervisor and managerial role, running the show and learning how to lead and train troops. The enlisted learn how to obey orders instantly and remain disciplined and fine-tuned. They are the dirty hands that do the work.

All pilots are officers, so I had stirred the wrong hornets' nest when asking the enlisted recruiters how to become an officer. The sergeants and staff sergeants at the office I visited began feeding me stories about how much better it was to enlist first, then go to college. Not only would school be paid for, they slyly said, but I would receive more respect when I became an officer. An officer who was an enlisted man first is known as a mustang.

All I had to do was become a non-commissioned officer and apply for the program. It made sense to me and at 18 years old, I began to play with the idea of enlisting instead of becoming an officer.

When one enlists, one may also secure a Military Occupational Specialty or MOS. An MOS serves as one's preliminary job and where a Marine will start training after Boot Camp. Many people don't immediately realize that any large body of troops requires a myriad of specialized supporting roles besides combat. The infantry get the job done that the Pentagon needs; securing a country, defending the territory, etc. While the infantry are undoubtedly the largest MOS in the USMC, the rest of the MOSs account for the majority of the Marine Corps. I don't know the actual statistic but I wouldn't be surprised if less than 20 percent of Marines are actual combat-seeking MOSs. The rest are clerks, truck drivers, aircraft mechanics, even air conditioner maintenance.

Think of it this way; a football team consists of roughly 45 players on offense, defense, special teams, and substitutions. But think of the hundreds that support them; not only the coaches, owners, managers, and publicists but also the Gatorade mixers, jersey-makers, bus drivers, etc.

The recruiting office where I was located was run by infantry Marines. I was considering artillery and intelligence, citing my ease for math and numbers. However, the recruiters told me that at the moment, the USMC didn't need any artillery-men or intelligence Marines. Instead (go figure) the USMC needed a few ground-pounding infantry devil dogs or tankers. Tankers were bullet magnets, the recruiters coerced, and I would be much happier sleeping on the ground than in a tank. I understood from them that after I enlisted, I would spend only a few months in the service and then I would return to college to secure a commission. I thought I was headed for a fast track to a cockpit. It didn't seem to matter what MOS I picked from the way they explained it, so I signed the dotted line.

So the reason I tell people that I joined the USMC, is because I wanted to fly, yada yada yada. However, there are other underlying psychological reasons that I've noticed since leaving the Corps.

In high school, drinking and smoking was 'cool'. I was not 'cool' in high school since I did not drink or smoke weed. Apparently, volunteering not to break the law was portrayed as a weakness and I believed what others believed of me; that I was weak. I was wiry, small, and had a timid demeanor.

I distinctly remember one dinner a few days before I left for Boot Camp. My family and I were sitting outside around a wooden table and the conversation moved to my impending departure. I had shaved my head and begun training at this point. I had read a few books on training at Boot Camp and while I was still mostly in the dark, I was very much in the mindset to leave. My family looked at me and began trying to reassure me that failure was OK because Boot Camp was going to be the hardest thing I would ever do. They were trying to be kind and prepare my natural optimism for a let down.

Failure was an option. Not only was it an option, but it was a strong possibility. This mentality was the weakness I faced in myself and what others saw in me. People saw me as someone who had a good heart and outward personality but was book smart. Perhaps I was not ready for the challenges of the world, let alone the rigors of a military training camp; especially not one run by Marines. Even as foreigners, my family understood that the Marines were tough.

The fact that I was the type of person who may fail frustrated me, and I got up and left the table determined to prove them wrong. My family was not cruel; they just didn't know that they were becoming a manifestation of the hurdles I was overcoming. Up until this point, I had never pushed myself to any limits and no one had any reason to believe there was any hidden strength or determination inside me.

Despite my determination, I had only a vague notion of what I was signing up for. I understood the commitment and responsibility, but not the impact that the USMC would have on my life. I joined to prove to everyone (especially myself) that I could stand with the ranks of hardened killers and hold my head up. I had to prove to myself I was not as weak as others believed me to be.

My parents were upset with the idea that I was signing up for the military and believed that I had so much more potential. They asked me to start college and do at least one year before enlisting. They hoped that I would find a niche or a routine at school and forget all about enlisting.

So whether it was because I wanted to kill people, prove to myself and my family that I was a tough individual, or because of a childhood dream to fly jets, I enlisted in the USMC after a year of college. I was determined, and on May 9th, 2004 with a shaved head and nothing but the clothes on my back, I was dropped off at the recruiters' office to leave for Parris Island, South Carolina.

With my parents three days before Boot Camp

Boot Camp

The journey began with a drive to the Pennsylvania capital. After I put in my papers and got my information squared away, I stayed in a hotel with other young men and women all destined for different basic training branches. Not everyone was leaving for the USMC, and on a crammed taxi ride from the processing building, a conversation was initiated by a naïve young woman.

We were passing a truck stop and there were four of us in the taxi. I kept to myself; shy but also a little proud that I was the only Marine recruit in the car. The others began talking about the truckers sleeping in their cabs.

"I could never do that," said the girl disapprovingly in the front seat of the taxi. "You have to sleep in a truck and travel all day?"

"Yeah, they have no life and those guys are all losers," remarked one of the guys next to me, cynically.

"Oh yeah, it's much worse than travelling to some foreign country, sleeping on the ground, and killing everyone you meet," I responded sarcastically, looking out the window. I get frustrated when others mock or degrade something they are unaware of and in this case it was flat out ironic. The others stared at me and the conversation ebbed for the rest of the ride to the hotel. Idiots. The distinction between Marine recruits and the rest of the military recruits was becoming more apparent to me.

It is often portrayed that the drill instructors break you down at

Boot Camp and then build you back up into the person they need you to be. This portrayal is mostly the case. I say 'mostly' because I believe people who sign up for the military already possess a certain mindset. If a person has the fortitude to make a decision to serve their country knowing that there are risks, they are well on their way to becoming an outstanding military serviceman or woman. Furthermore, people who join the USMC know that it requires stamina to succeed and want to find the stamina within them. The key word here is 'find'; not 'create'. This inner strength can be grown and developed, but it has to be there in the first place.

I had no idea what my time in the military was going to be like, but I had visions of four years away from family and friends in a foreign country. Prior to my enlistment, I saw movies portraying a war hero succeeding, but the movie rarely showed a soldier or sailor returning home and experiencing all of the ordinary administrative tasks associated with any deployment. He often finishes a battle or overcomes a struggle and returns to base. Roll credits. As far as I knew, I was going to be overseas at war the entire time I was a Marine.

Another idea which I didn't learn until after leaving for the USMC was the idea of a skill-set Marine. Again, think of a Marine as a football player. Every player does a particular task from passing the ball, running, catching, or tackling the person with the ball, simply put.

Similarly, each MOS knows how to do a particular task such as blow things up, find criminals, ensure people get paid, or guard the president. Prior to Boot Camp, I saw every Marine as a super-disciplined killing machine. However, the super-disciplined Marines are the presidential guard, silent drill team, and pall bearers. The killing machines are the infantry, tanks, and of course, Reconnaissance Marines.

Just as each football player may be responsible in an emergency to tackle, pass, or run, each Marine is trained to shoot, drill, and perform as a war-fighter if only on a basic level. The USMC has a tenet that embodies this idea that says, "Every Marine, a rifleman."

From my encounter in the taxi, I was already beginning to realize the diversity of the military branches from the caliber of intelligence next to me. I fantasized that there would be no such idiots in the USMC and at Boot Camp. Every Marine was a super-disciplined killing machine, right?

After the brief, cheap stint in the hotel, we were taken to the airport where I boarded a flight for South Carolina with about ten other USMC recruits. We were all sitting in different places on the plane and even though we had exchanged brief salutations, I felt alone.

Once we disembarked from the plane we were ushered through the terminal to a little alcove and told to stand with our noses against the wall along with other young men already there. A Marine took a few guys at a time through a little door and I anxiously waited.

When my turn came, there were only twelve or so guys left and we were rushed through a side door in the airport down what felt like narrow basement corridors. It all felt so disorienting, which was the point. No one arrives at Boot Camp during the day, with the intention of adding to the element of shock when one turns up.

We waited in line outside a room with no idea what to expect. When one of the Marines came out, one of the guys spoke up.

"Sir, I need to go—," he began.

"Shut up out here! No one talks! Next!" the Marine responded, and the next guy went in the door. A few minutes later, the Marine came out again, took one look at the guy who had asked a question and exploded.

"Why the hell did you piss yourself?!" he demanded.

"Sir, I had to go to the bathroom really badly," the young man sheepishly replied, now with a giant wet mark on the front of his pants.

"Well why didn't you ask, dipshit?" the Marine asked incredulously.

"Sir, you didn't let me talk."

Ordinarily, this scenario would have been funny. But with all the confusion and anticipation, I was more worried about myself and what lay ahead, than if someone else pissed himself.

The Marines put us on a bus and drove us over one group at a time. When it came for my turn to get on the bus, there were only a handful of us still waiting. We got on and I volunteered to wake everyone up when we got to the island. I was so stressed and anxious that I couldn't imagine sleeping even a couple of seconds.

As everyone nodded off, I stared out the window feeling more alone and anxious than ever before. I had no toiletries, no clothes, and no personal belongings. The lights came on just as we pulled up and the doors opened ominously at the famous yellow footprints painted on the ground. No one moved.

I had heard about the drill instructors (DI) from movies and legend but had not seen any in person. The Marines in the airport didn't wear the wide brimmed smokey hats that distinguish DIs so they might not have been drill instructors. When the doors opened, the first drill instructor I ever saw stormed onto the bus and began to explain the routine.

"Listen up, knuckleheads! You are on my island. This is my bus. You are mine now. You do everything I say as soon as I say it, you understand?" Spit flecked from his mouth as the veins in his neck strained to send blood to his brain. One recruit volunteered a quiet "yes, sir."

"I said, 'DO YOU UNDERSTAND!?' WHEN I ASK YOU A QUESTION, YOU SAY 'YES, SIR'. WHEN I GIVE YOU AN ORDER, YOU ANSWER, 'AYE, SIR'. DO YOU UNDERSTAND?"

"YES, SIR!" we yelled in hesitation. He was clearly pissed at us and I had no idea what we had done.

"Now get off my bus, you have thirty seconds twenty-ninetwenty-eighttwenty-seven—" We ran off the bus onto the footprints as he counted at lightening speed and into the building to begin processing.

As long as I did not attract the immediate attention of a drill instructor, I didn't feel any pressure or concern. It was when I went too slow or did something incorrectly that angst started to increase. I am a pretty sharp guy so I avoided the constant gaze of the DIs for the most part. This method is called being the gray man.

The idea behind being the gray man is to never fail, but never to succeed beyond what is expected. It is perfect for going unnoticed, but it also prevents one from achieving recognition.

During processing we called our families and read from a card taped onto a wall. It was 2:00 am when we called and told them that we had arrived safely, not to call back, and that they would receive mail and our address shortly. Click . That was the end of the call. Any chance of a cry for help was stifled by the fear of the angry man behind me. My parents told me later that my voice was already sore and croaky when I called, just a few short minutes into Parris Island.

Next came the "moment of truth" where they tried to weed out people who lied on their enlistment papers. The DI scared us into believing that they had advanced DNA techniques of finding out who had done drugs exactly on which date. Now was the time to fess up and no harm would come to us. I stuck around in order to explain a recent surgery on my eye lid that I had left unrecorded. Next to me, a kid told the DI that he'd like to change the number of times he'd smoked pot from four to something higher.

"Well what would you like to change it to?" a DI snapped in his face, holding pen to paper.

"A lot, sir!" barked back the recruit, staring straight ahead.

"Well, I need a number, shit-stick! How often did you smoke pot?"

"Every day for five years, sir," replied the recruit with obvious consternation and noticeably quieter.

"I can't write that, retard! Give me a number. A hundred? A thousand?"

"Nine hundred and ninety-nine thousand, nine hundred and ninety-nine, SIR!"

The drill instructor just stared at this kid and I'm sure more than a few smiles broke out. The DI shook his head and moved on. This guy would have to wait. Somehow, idiots had followed me here to Boot Camp. I explained my problem and moved on without a hassle.

The recruits arriving with me were put in 3rd Battalion, M Co. (or Mike Company). Six platoons were formed from the 400 recruits. A platoon was made up of about 60 recruits from all over the eastern U.S. There is another Boot Camp on the west coast that serves everyone roughly west of the Mississippi river.

For the first couple days of Boot Camp, we were put in a holding platoon where we learned how to make our beds properly, the basics of marching, how to pack our foot lockers, and other little details. We were all new to Parris Island except for two recruits who joined us, recently healed from injuries; D'Errico and Thomas.

David D'Errico was placed in charge of the platoon. He had been in Boot Camp for a few weeks and re-cycled to heal from his injuries. He was a six foot, strongly built, Puerto Rican who hailed from Florida. As he badgered and squared away the other recruits in the platoon, I knew I hated him.

I served as late chow recruit during my time at Boot Camp. This duty meant that while everyone else went to eat, I stayed behind with another recruit to watch the rifles that were locked up. Two other recruits, dubbed early chow, went to chow ahead of the platoon and when early chow came back to replace us, we ate breakfast, lunch, or dinner and met up with our platoon afterwards.

It was during my first late chow duty that the Company Gunnery Sergeant came on deck. This Marine was a DI in charge of all the other DIs in Mike Company. Not knowing our duties within a few days of arriving, the other recruit on late chow and I were sitting down and talking. The gunny lit into us, yelling about how we were supposed to be patrolling the squad bay and explained our responsibilities.

After he left, I expected that the punishment was over, but I was sorely mistaken. That evening, the entire company was called into one of the squad bays to learn how to perform the exercises that we would be doing each morning. The Company Gunny gave a simple demonstration on each, followed by the proper commands to yell at the beginning and end of each exercise.

"Now. Let me have the four recruits that I caught on late chow sitting down. You know who you are," the Company Gunny said, looking out over the faces. Two other recruits from another platoon had been caught sitting down as well. We moved through the recruits sitting Indian style until we stood in a line facing the Gunny in front of everyone else. My gray man technique wasn't working.

"I'm going to give you exercises, and you're going to do the exercises until I say stop. When I say stop, yell the proper response. Understood?" the DI said staring at us with arms crossed.

"AYE, SIR!" We chorused.

"Run in place."

"RUN IN PLACE, AYE SIR!"

"Knees higher."

"KNEES HIGHER, AYE SIR!"

"Knees higher."

"KNEES HIGHER, AYE SIR!"

"Pushups."

"PUSHUPS, AYE SIR!"

"Down."

"ONE!"

"Down."

"TWO!"

The DI cycled through the exercises one at a time, moving from one to the next. He gave the commands almost casually as we screamed the responses. We jumped, ran, pushed, and strained as best as we could while yelling the appropriate commands when asked. Recruits looked on in horror.

After what felt like an eternity, the DI told us to stop. We yelled our response and the DI looked us over. We stood there, chests heaving, sweat dripping, as we waited for the verdict.

"You three may sit down. You," he said, pointing at me as the other recruits made there way to the back of the crowd. "Stay here. Jumping jacks."

I couldn't believe it. I hadn't done anything different than the other three. I had no idea why I was being singled out but here I was jumping, pushing, and running alone. I was clearly making a mistake but I didn't know what it was.

"Stop," the DI commanded.

"STOP, AYE SIR!" I yelled back in response.

"Run in place."

"RUN IN PLACE, AYE SIR!"

"Stop," the DI intoned after only a few moments of running. I realized I was not responding to the end of the exercise correctly so I tried different approaches.

"STOP, SIR!" I ventured.

"Pushups."

"PUSHUPS, AYE SIR!" and I began pushing again.

"Stop."

"AYE, SIR! STOP, SIR!" I guessed. This continued and after several minutes, the other recruits began visibly shaking their heads. Some even spoke up to give me the answer but I couldn't hear what they were mumbling over the sound of my feet slapping the ground.

"Stop, recruit," the DI said, shaking his head.

"STOP, GOOD MORNING, SIR!" I screamed frantically.

"The correct response is 'stop, aye, sir. Good morning, sir'," the DI said, clearly at the end of his patience. "Now get back in formation and sit down."

I made my way back into the company dripping with sweat. People turned to watch me as I sat down. I was exhausted.

Late chow afforded me with lots of time away from the DIs who were busy with the rest of the platoon. The free-time allowed me to get rid of contraband such as candy wrappers and extra mail that other recruits had. My fellow late chow recruit and I were away from the watchful eye of the DI and had the liberty to talk and relax a little while we counted rifles, secured locks, and watched the squad bay.

One day, several weeks into Boot Camp, D'Errico received a box of power bars during mail call. We were allowed to receive cough drops and power bars but they would be kept by the drill instructors and divvied out to the platoon as a whole.

D'Errico had a knack for breaking or bending the rules. He excelled at everything he did, simply by believing that he was better. If someone ran fast, D'Errico had to run faster. If someone had extra free time to write letters, D'Errico wanted equal free time. And if he received power bars in the mail, all those power bars were his by right.

That evening, sometime before we had to get in bed, D'Errico snuck into the DI's office and took back the box of power bars that had been sent to him. This act was beyond criminal. D'Errico and I had become bunk mates towards the back of the squad bay and during our conversations together, we had become good friends. As I lay in bed trying to fall asleep, a hand crept around the edge of the bed and offered me some power bars.

As we tore open the wrappers, we coughed to mask the sound of the plastic. It was a futile effort and we knew everyone else heard it. The next day, D'Errico was fingered by someone else in the platoon and he was asked to dump his foot locker and sea bag. As the DIs went through all his possessions my blood pressure rose. I had already disposed of the wrapper evidence during late chow but we would be caught if they found the remaining power bars.

But D'Errico had already thought of this. During the night, realizing he would be caught, he ate the rest of the box. The DIs were furious but had no certainty that he had actually done it. Instead, they moved our beds right up front next to the DI office where they could keep an eye on us, especially D'Errico.

I used to sleep walk and sleep talk notoriously as a child and Boot Camp was no different. I never remembered the different episodes, but other recruits shot dirty looks at me. When I slept walked, I woke others up with my yelling and moving around the squad bay.

One evening, after the DIs had left the squad bay, I sat bolt upright in bed. I was on the top bunk so I jumped to the next top bunk and yelled, "Cover and align, shift on down the line!"

The guy in the next bunk fell off onto the floor and recruits woke up and stared. The next morning as we stood to attention, recruits glared at me. I had no idea what was going on until my late chow companion told me.

During every waking and sleeping moment the DIs had control over our activities. They rotated during the night shift so there was always a DI on duty. We did everything by the number, even brushing our teeth. The DIs would tell us to brush the left side of our teeth and gave us a count of ten seconds. Then the right side. We followed orders for everything from tying a specific shoe lace to buttoning certain buttons. This strict obedience to orders taught us discipline and any slip up in following directions earned us a stint in the pit or on the quarterdeck.

The pits are scattered around Parris Island. They are large boxes of sand that can hold an entire platoon. If a DI wanted a recruit to really suffer, the recruit was brought to the pit. The sand fleas, heat, and sand all contributed to the misery of the pit.

The quarterdeck was a part of the squad bay closest to the drill instructors' office. The quarterdeck was where recruits received their mail, studied knowledge, and paid for their mistakes. The pits were painful because of the biting sand fleas and intense heat. The quarterdeck was bad because it was out of the public eye and there was no leash on the DI punishment.

My platoon had four DIs. There were three regular DIs and one senior DI who was in charge of the platoons progress. Each DI was assigned a specific task and element of training. Sergeant (Sgt) Watson was our kill hat. The kill hat is the DI with the biggest attitude. He's the one who advocates all the recruits being in the pit. Watson also led us in marching or drill.

Sgt Gavilanes taught knowledge and the USMC academic work. He also doubled as a kill hat. If the other two DIs left us alone with Watson and Gavilanes, we knew we were in for a rough night.

Staff Sgt (SSgt) Murphy was the opposite of Gavilanes and Watson. He saved us from the other two kill hats on many occasions. He oversaw the instructors and trained us on the rifle range.

Lastly, our senior drill instructor was SSgt Ford. He performed the administrative tasks and we regarded him like our father. He passed out the mail and didn't get too hands-on in training except to motivate us. He had the final say in all instruction.

Early on in Boot Camp, the DIs began conditioning us for combat. With every lunge during martial arts training we screamed, "KILL!" When I waited to enter the ring with the pugil sticks, the DI encouraged me to destroy the opponent. The ditties we sang as we ran involved death, casualties, and the glory of killing the enemy or not coming home at all. This brainwashing all began to sink in with regularity.

We trained to follow orders to the letter, immediately, and without hesitation. Even dressing in the beginning of Boot Camp started by button, by boot, by trouser leg. If someone went a button too fast or put on the wrong boot, everyone took off their clothes and started over.

During the entire three months of making a Marine, we referred to ourselves in the third person. Every request was phrased, "Recruit Vandekar requests permission to..." or "This recruit needs to go..."

This process took away the mentality that we had any freedoms; even the freedom to be an individual.

Initially I got my own tasks done and stood proudly showing the drill instructor how much faster I was than everyone else, but I quickly learned that this was an individual mindset. If someone made a mistake, often times the drill instructors would punish everyone or at least everyone around the error. Getting done early didn't do anyone any good. One succeeds in Boot Camp by finishing quickly, then turning to others and helping them. We became a unit and shed our individualism.

One of the most prominent lessons in Boot Camp involved our rifles. We learned how to take apart rifles and how to shoot for proficiency. One of the Marine Corps' policies is that every Marine is a rifleman first. This mantra means that unlike other branches, every Marine learns to shoot and acts like the infantry if only on a basic level.

I had never shot a gun before, but at Boot Camp I excelled at shooting. The rifle creed ("This is my rifle. There are many like it but this one is mine...") was grilled into our heads and before bed each night we screamed it at the top of our lungs, ending the creed by pounding our beds three times. Picture it: 60 young men yelling about the possessiveness of their weapons and then pounding their beds with fists. We could hear when other platoons were going to bed by the thumping and muffled yells.

One of the most intimidating events at Boot Camp was the gas chamber. To fleet Marines, the chamber has lost all its potency; units are required to go to the gas chamber every six months as a refresher. However, in Boot Camp when we headed there for the first time, the term "gas chamber" implied death and torment.

My platoon filed into a small 25' square room, keeping to the edges of the wall and standing in little boxes painted to the floor. As we peered through our gas masks we could see that the room had no paint on the walls and was bare except for a table with a contraption in the center with a Marine in a gas mask standing next to it. There were no windows and two doors; the one we came in and the door we would leave through. We had learned to don and clear our gas masks prior to entering, but this would show us if we had learned correctly.

Once everyone was in a spot on the wall, evenly spaced, they introduced a CS tablet into the contraption. Pale white smoke curled upward but because we had our gas masks on, we initially felt nothing. Our DIs paced in front of us, watching our hands and eyes to make sure no one was panicking.

CS gas, or tear gas, is lethally harmless. Symptoms include a running nose full of mucus, tears streaming from the eyes, coughing, burning in the nose and throat areas, disorientation, dizziness and restricted breathing. Typically anywhere there is moisture, it will hurt. It will also burn the skin where there is sweat or sunburn. After a few minutes outside in fresh air, the effects begin to wear off.

"Ladies," shouted the Marine in the center. "For the first part, you will bend at the waist and shake your head in a rigorous motion." We complied as our DIs paced the room, looking for people who were succumbing to the gas and pressure. This step ensured our masks were properly worn and sealed. It also gave us confidence that our masks would not fall off.

"For the next step," the Marine in the center barked once he had our attention again. "Place two fingers underneath your mask and break the seal. Keep your eyes closed and hold your breath. Once we tell you, take your fingers out and clear your mask."

This procedure would allow gas to penetrate the seal. We would then clear our mask by expelling air quickly, open our eyes, and continue breathing. One by one we did this without any problems. Some people began to cough a little. Once we opened our eyes in our masks, I noticed they had begun to sting, but nothing any more serious than cutting an onion.

Once all the recruits had settled and were breathing, the Marine gave us the last command.

"Lastly, you are going to loosen the straps of your mask, place the mask on top of your head, turn to your left, and exit the chamber in an orderly single-file line." This step required more patience and practice but wasn't very difficult for most.

As we waited with the masks on our heads, eyes screwed shut, and holding our breath, one recruit somehow got a lungful of gas. He began hacking, clawing, and fighting his way to the door. The DIs pressed him against a wall to get his mask on his face.

Outside, the effects of tear gas burned our lungs and eyes. The DIs made us walk around in circles with our arms out to prevent us from scratching our faces and increasing the irritation. It is not fun to get hit with CS gas.

During pool week, the DIs tested us in four different swim qualifications, beginning with the easiest at number four. The fourth qualification (Combat Water Survival or CWS-4) involved basic swimming techniques and floating in the water. The third, CWS-3, involved strapping a helmet and flak jacket on and swimming with a rifle a certain distance. CWS-2 was a little tougher with longer distances and jumping from a high dive into the water. It also involved towing a Marine in the water. Finally, CWS-1 involved rescuing a distressed swimmer who attempted to drown us from several positions, demonstrating all the swimming techniques, and swimming 250 meters. Few Marines made it to CWS-1 and even fewer passed. I attempted CWS-1 with D'Errico, but only he passed.

There were three phases to Boot Camp and each one was marked by an improvement in uniform standards. During the first stage, recruits wore "go-fasters" or sneakers and a yellow glow belt around their body like a sash. They had their pants unrolled at the bottom and no names on their green camouflage uniforms.

During the second stage, recruits transitioned to the rifle range and began to wear tan uniforms. This change in uniform gave us our first air of seniority and we began to look at other recruits with contempt. We also started marching in boots. The boots made our platoon a lot louder during marches and the drill instructors began shouting, "Let me hear that THUNDER!"

During the last and final stage of Boot Camp we wore our green uniforms again but this time they had our last name on one side of the chest and U.S. Marines on the other. The first time I looked down and saw VANDEKAR side by side with U.S. Marines I felt a swelling of pride. I was the first Vandekar to wear a U.S. military uniform.

During the third phase, we also began to roll our trouser legs into boot bands which gave us a more military appearance. When we marched to the barber shop, instead of shaving our heads bald, we received a high and tight haircut. At this point, we absolutely looked at every other recruit on the island as junior to us and therefore inferior. We looked like Marines.

In fact, the DIs made us unroll our trouser legs or wear go-fasters when we disappointed them, therefore "demoting" our platoon to an earlier phase and embarrassing us. We wanted nothing more, as recruits, but to roll our trousers up like Marines. Ironically, in a Marine Reconnaissance unit, team members are always unrolling their trousers in order to appear less uniform.

During Boot Camp, we were essentially cutoff from the outside with no idea of what was happening in the news. To learn our academic work, we marched over the base to the auditorium where we took our seats and were lectured about Marine Corps heroes, wars, and tactics.

As we learned Marine Corps history, we were ignorant to current events. At the beginning of one history lecture, the DIs came in with breaking news in the world; North Korea had just invaded South Korea. Shock rippled through us. The DI told us that everyone would be skipping pool week, moving straight to the rifle range and out of boot camp to infantry units to deploy to Korea. It didn't matter what our MOS was. If anyone wanted to see the chaplain, now was the time.

Hands shot into the air to get right with God and one of the recruits next to me said to anyone who would listen, "This is messed up! I'm Korean! I'm Korean!"

We filed out of the auditorium and stood around chattering to each other. The DIs then herded us right back in where they let us in on reality. All was right in the world. The only war we would go to was Afghanistan or Iraq and he yelled words that I never forgot. "Let me shit you straight, knuckleheads; 100 percent of you are going to Iraq!"

Boot Camp was mentally fatiguing. At the time it was physically difficult because I had never pushed my body to any sort of extremes but a fit athlete would not have been alien to the workouts. The only shock was the 24-hour surveillance the DI had on us. They appeared inhuman as they rotated shifts, never eating or sleeping in our presence.

On another aspect, almost everything I did was learned. I had never marched before and we never went anywhere without marching. When we waited in lines for the barber, we yelled history, creeds, and general orders. We broke down our rifles over and over and over until it became second nature. We fought each other in martial arts and swam with rifles and packs. It was all foreign and my brain struggled to process it all.

The team state of mind was the mentality that gave me the pride I was seeking. When I graduated Boot Camp, I don't know if I had the self-confidence that I sought, but I was proud of the team I had joined. I had not done anything to earn honor but I had been accepted into the ranks of those who had. I was not a veteran but Marines were the finest fighting force in the world.

People had disbelieved I would succeed. I had doubted my own strength and yet, on graduation day, Sgt Watson stood in front of me, handed me an Eagle, Globe, and Anchor, and said, "Well done, Marine."

The Recon Screening

I still had no idea what the Marine Corps was like. We were given ten days of leave or vacation after Boot Camp and as far as I knew, the rest of the next three years and nine months was going to be filled with angry sergeants and pissed off people telling me exactly where to go and how to sleep.

Now that I was a Marine, the next step in my training was the School of Infantry or SOI. This school is reserved for Marines going specifically into the infantry. Duh! All the other MOSs go to a summarized version of SOI called Marine Combat Training or MCT. If you're having trouble with the acronyms, refer to the back of the book.

In SOI and MCT, Marines learn to dig fighting holes, conduct squad rushes, shoot all kinds of weapons, and a little land navigation. There is plenty more that we learn, of course, but it comes down to just a few basic tactics. The school encompasses two and a half months.

The instructors at SOI didn't treat us poorly like the DIs did during Boot Camp, which was a surprise. They talked to us like regular people with an emphasis on respect. After all, we were Marines now, just like them. The school class was about 250 people compared to the 60 in a platoon at Boot Camp, but this number varies by the season. The company was split alphabetically into two platoons. D'Errico had come to SOI as well but was put into 1st Platoon.

Initially, everyone at SOI learns the different infantry tactics and attends classes together for about two weeks. After this period, each person picks an MOS specialty within infantry that they'd like to be. The USMC gives SOI a number of required mortar-men, machine gunners, riflemen, etc. and the instructors award us our choices based on our class standing. After that point, each MOS trains independently.

Every MOS in the USMC is given a four number designator with the first two numbers being the general field and the last two being the specialty within that field. For infantry, the first two numbers are 03xx. A rifleman is an 0311; machine gunner is 0331; mortar-man is 0341; assault-man 0351; and a tow gunner is 0352. However, all 03's are called grunts. Now this breakdown raises many questions in your mind so before I go any further let me burn off that fog.

A rifleman is the basic infantry marine. He digs holes, carries an M16 (typically), and does the Marine Corps dirty work. The machine gunner is more specialized but works closely with the rifleman. The machine gunner, of course, uses the USMC machine guns such as the M240b, MK19, and M2. The mortar-man uses mortars (a long-range indirect-fire weapon) to lob explosive rounds at the enemy. The assault-man uses the rocket launcher as his weapon of choice and this MOS was incidentally my first pick. Lastly, the tow gunner uses vehicle-mounted large rockets to inflict massive hate and discontent across the battlefield.

You may have noticed a jump from 0311 to 0331. 0321 (said oh-three-twenty-one) is reserved for the most coveted of Marine Corps billets: the Reconnaissance Marine. As a special operations asset, he uses every weapon, trains in multiple special insert schools, learns to inflict massive damage through support-by-fire, or sits back and observes the enemy with high-powered sniper rifles and optics. We'll get into all that later.

When picking our infantry specialized roles, we were told there was a limited availability for each slot. If we passed the Recon screening, we would train to become 0321s at a different school. Those who were attempting to become 0321s, were not going to get mortar training (0341) if someone else wanted it. Therefore, the Marines who passed the Recon screening would be trained through SOI as 0311s.

During my first few weeks at infantry school, before we had chosen MOSs, a Recon Marine came in to brief us on the 0321 MOS and the Reconnaissance Community. Only SOI Marines get the opportunity to join Recon before entering the fleet, the term used to describe being assigned to an active unit. The other MOSs go through MCT and then train at their MOS school (engineering, communications, intelligence, etc.). These Marines are given the chance to take the Recon screening once they have joined their unit in the fleet.

As we stood in formation one day, the instructors read off the names that qualified to listen to the briefing. These names included Marines who had swum well and performed a 1st class Physical Fitness Test (PFT) at Boot Camp. It also required a USMC test entry score of 105 and U.S. citizenship. While I was sure that I qualified for all the requirements, I knew I was not a U.S. citizen, and therefore my name was not on the list.

D'Errico had qualified to listen to the brief and we stuck pretty close so I felt a need to be there. I had begun to pass boundaries in Boot Camp that I never knew existed in my own mind and I knew Recon was elite, even though I didn't know exactly what it was.

I approached the Gunnery Sergeant who had read off the names. "Gunny, I was not on your list but I have a first class PFT and passed the swim qualifications. I am not on your list because I was born in England. I'm not a U.S. citizen, but I'm about to get it."

"Come on in," he replied. "If you pass the screening, we'll deal with your citizenship later."

There were roughly fifty of us in that room. I could tell something different was happening because they closed the doors and made sure no one was outside. I had gone through something this secret when going through presidential guard selection but that position was ceremonial; this one was clearly more dangerous. Recon Marines aren't the USMC prized show horses – they're the sharks.

The Gunny stood in front of us and paused for effect. "Being a Recon Marine is all the things you hear the Marine Corps doing. We're the guys kicking in doors and jumping out of helicopters. We're the snipers and raiders coming out of the water with dive gear. We are the best of the best.

"We're looking for a mentality. You're not in shape to pass Recon school now. But when we ask you to run 15 miles and you can only run 9, we want the guy who runs to his limit and passes out. Not the Marine who gives up when he realizes he won't make it.

"You've already achieved so much by joining the Marine Corps and passing Boot Camp. All of you here have excelled in PT, the pool, and your test scores. You're well on your way to a successful career in the military regardless of if you pass Recon or not. But if you choose, this is the next level up. This is the varsity team.

"Next Friday at 0500 there will be a bus waiting out front to take you to the Recon screening. If you want to try out, you will be excused from SOI physical training (PT)."

He left the room with us sitting there in our own fantasy worlds. I had no idea what Reconnaissance was specifically, but I had an understanding that it was challenging.

An infantry school instructor came in after the briefing and waited for the Gunny to leave. We knew very little about our instructors. He began by telling us that he had been in a sniper unit before becoming an SOI instructor and if we wanted to be the top, we wanted to be Recon. I had heard this boast four times now, like you have read, and it was starting to resonate in a thick, jarhead skull.

Friday came around, and clambering onto the bus were 22 students who all wanted to attempt the screening from the 50 or so who heard the brief. I didn't know what would take place, but we chatted about what we expected. Some people didn't care if they made it or not; they just wanted to give it a shot. Others had read about Recon their whole lives, had dreamed about it, and it was the reason they joined the USMC. I knew D'Errico well, but most of the other people I had just met at SOI and were a little unfamiliar.

It was a mix of small skinny frames (myself included) and big thick meatheads. Society tells you that appearance is what matters, that the big guys are the strong ones. Naturally, I believed it would be the six biggest guys on the bus who would pass and the rest of us would go back to being regular Marines. I was a little leary that I would make it, but the Recon Marine had told us that they were looking for willpower, determination, and the drive to succeed despite the costs. I had perseverance and I was going to give it my best.

We got off the bus in PT gear: go-fasters, short shorts, and a t-shirt. The Marine Corps mostly wears green shorts and a green shirt. However, Recon Marines wear the coveted black shorts earned at Amphibious Reconnaissance School. It differentiates them from other units and is a source of pride.

We had brought along a pair of camouflage utilities (camis) on request and found that we had been dropped off at the base pool. We were herded into the bleachers where they briefed us on the screening that was to take place. As we waited to hear what we would be doing, my feet were tapping on the bleachers. I had never tried out for anything and never pushed myself, and as I sat there,

I got very nervous. A few other Marines from the fleet had joined us in their chance to take the Recon screening as well, and we all huddled up to listen to the demands.

The Recon Marine who had briefed us at SOI was giving us the summary of our screening while three other Recon Marines stood by, nonchalant and cocky. They looked no bigger or smaller than any other Marine but they exhibited an air of confidence that made them appear intimidating and fearful. They didn't appear undisciplined, but they weren't rigid like the Marines who had trained me thus far.

"Alright, listen up," began the Gunny. Even in his dialogue, he gave off an air of informality but authority. No one had been talking so he continued.

"After we finish the briefing, you'll have five minutes to change into your cami tops and bottoms in the locker rooms behind me. Make sure you shower off and line up on the side of the pool at the top of the deep end.

"The screening will start with a 500 meter swim for time. After the distance swim, you'll perform a crossover or underwater swim followed by a rifle carry. After this, you'll tread water and then we'll leave the pool and do a standard PFT out here on the road. You'll need to score a first class PFT as well as pass all the other events in order to qualify for Recon training.

"These Marines behind me will be assisting you on the different tasks and performing the safety swimmer functions. Now, you have the choice of doing the PFT first or the swim portion."

Everyone unanimously voted for the swim portion first. We all knew what was included in a PFT and we wanted to tackle the unknown without being weary or fatigued from a run. We filed out of the bleachers and into the locker rooms to get changed.

The screening began with a simple 500 meter swim in under twelve minutes; easy enough. However, it had to be done in camis. Around 30 of us hit the water and began swimming the 50 meter pool, bumping into each other as some outpaced the others. As we began to space out, swimming in opposite directions, we would collide with each other. With our heads down, we would inadvertently smack into someone who was coming the other way. This inconvenience increased the frustration and killed our stride. I am not a fast swimmer, but I am comfortable in the water. Being comfortable in the water is important to a Recon Marine.

Next was a crossover. A crossover involves swimming the width of the pool (25 meters) underwater. Again, this exercise was to be done in camis. The crossover is not excruciatingly difficult if done right. The trick to crossovers is to head to the bottom of the pool and swim with your head down. The second a Marine looks up and judges the distance, he starts to think he doesn't have enough air and gets the temptation to head to the surface. A few people had dropped from the 500 meter swim and two or three more failed the crossover.

After the crossover, we had to swim a rifle across the width of the pool, keeping the rifle above the water. At the other side of the 25 meters we had to tread water for ten seconds with the rifle held in both hands above our head; taxing, but not impossible. However, with all these events back-to-back, fatigue had begun to set in.

Eleven people remained in what I thought was the most difficult part: the confined tread. In this exercise, everyone was shepherded into the deep end where we treaded water, still in camis. We were pressed chest-to-back with no room for our arms or legs in a tight knit circle. Inevitably, I got knocked down below the others and kicked by flailing feet. I began to panic and claw my way to the surface through the thrashing limbs, unable to find the hole that I had sunk from.

The moment I found the surface, it became a struggle to stay up with no room to move my arms or legs. Shoulders jutted into faces as we floundered in the turbulent water for some purchase to stay afloat. People gasped for air as we looked around for something, anything to reassure us we would be okay. One second I was on the surface, the next I was underwater again.

Meanwhile, the Recon Marines swam around the group like sharks, pushing them in tighter. People on the outside instinctively wanted to push away from the group or at least face outwards so they could use their arms. The Recon Marines forced these Marines inwards and swam underneath the group, dragging people under by their feet. This maneuver is called "sharking," and when I found myself surprisingly comfortable for a minute or two, that is most likely when I got sharked.

The Recon Marines also splashed water into the faces of the outside ring. Consequently, the outside with its comfort away from writhing bodies struggling to stay afloat, became fraught with splashing, turbulent water and just as difficult to breathe or see.

This tread went on for thirty minutes. There was a bell on the side sitting next to all the Marines who had quit so far. Anyone was allowed to leave the group by ringing the bell. Ringing the bell was a conscious sign that someone had given up and didn't "accidentally" swim out of the confined tread. People who had already failed the 500 meter swim or the crossover looked on with relief that they did not get to this stage.

The group started off, much like Boot Camp, with every man for himself. Everyone was kicking, thrashing and flailing, unable to stay afloat long enough to get a deep lung full of air. No techniques were established because no one had ever done something like this before. We were not allowed to talk or we would fail. Without communication and with fear on every face, I found myself on the verge of giving up. My cami top bunched up around my chest under my arms, restricting my movement. As I kicked to stay up, my trousers hindered my legs. I was panicking and could not go on.

I looked at my best friend, D'Errico, and saw him steadfastly treading water. Knowing him from Boot Camp, I knew his pride would not allow him to give up while others persisted, and so I found in myself the courage to continue as well.

Looking back at a simple training exercise like this one, I understand that there was no fear of drowning. Though it may have felt like absolute panic and horror, there was a safety vehicle nearby and the Recon Marines were there as safety swimmers primarily. Nevertheless, I was inexperienced and afraid. I was surrounded by people I had met a few weeks ago and each of us was attempting to stay afloat by pushing others down.

As the clock continued, we began to work as a team. As someone in the center lost their space to tread and went under, we would grab his elbow and pull him up, sending ourselves under instead. It was easier to be underwater if we had done it on purpose. Small communications began in the form of simple nods and murmured thank-you's. We were not allowed to wear watches in order to disorient ourselves from the time, but we began to feel that we could succeed.

Only two people got out during the confined tread. The confined tread hadn't weeded out anyone weak or strong physically. It had just separated those who would panic under stress, and those who were as comfortable in the water as they were on land.

The screening instructor finally told us to spread out, arms-width apart, and continue treading water. Still in our camis, we were told to remove our trousers and tie the legs together in a knot. By swinging the waist portion from behind our heads to the front, we would scoop air into the trousers. The trouser legs tied together would trap the air and a make-shift life-vest was made. If we could succeed in making one of these life-vests and float for another two minutes without treading water, we would be finished the pool phase.

Making a floatation device was a technique to master and if one could tread water and tie a knot, it was a simple task. I climbed out of the pool relieved that it was done. However, there was still a standard USMC PFT to run, complete with a qualifying score.

A USMC PFT is comprised of pull-ups, sit-ups, and a 3-mile run. Each portion is 1/3 of a total score of 300; 100 each. Twenty pull-ups, 100 crunches, and an 18 minute 3-mile run will get you that perfect 300. That means each pull-up is worth five points, each crunch is worth one point and each minute of the run is worth six points (or ten seconds is worth one point). There are techniques to improve a score but it breaks down to a simple assumption; it is easier to get five crunches or one pull-up, than shave fifty seconds off the run time. Work on the pull-ups and crunches.

Nine of us started pull-ups for the PFT. My arms felt like jelly from treading water and swimming the last hour. As I strained and groaned, I only achieved 13 for a total of 65 points. It was under par.

I never had any problem with crunches, achieving 100 this time around as well. My score so far was 165 points. Going into the run, my mind tried to calculate how fast I needed to run but I couldn't think clearly.

We began the run and I finished as fast as I could but with my legs as sore as my arms, I wasn't happy with my speed. We ran on a 1.5 mile course so as we looped around and passed each other, we offered encouragement.

The screening instructor tallied up our score. We needed a 225 or higher to pass. As he called off our scores, it was agonizing to wait to see if I had passed the pool but failed the PFT. I had no idea where I stood and my mind was fatigued. I couldn't do the math quick enough to work out if I was close or not.

"Vandekar – 246."

I was relieved. I had made it through Boot Camp and now passed the Recon Screening as well. One of the Marines, a tall guy named Gantz, had finished close to last on the run and failed the PFT. However, he had done extremely well in the water. The screening instructor asked if he had tried his hardest. Gantz shrugged and said "I guess." This answer wasn't what the Recon Marine was looking for and Gantz was cut from the list.

Those of us who passed filed back onto the bus and the others waiting there congratulated us. It surprised me to see guys much bigger than myself sitting down, and I'm sure it surprised them too. It was the beginning of a mindset which I learned; it's not the size of the man that determines his worth. Some of these bigger guys either had not been able to swim or were unwilling to push themselves past a certain point.

Despite being physically weaker (I believed), I had achieved what they could not. Yet this test was only the beginning. The screening only weeded out the people who qualified to train for Recon school. I was not an 0321 and there was a lot more PT between me and the title of Recon Marine.

As SOI continued, the other students would mock Recon to downplay our achievement. Regardless, those of us who had passed the screening felt proud of what we had done and when we saw one another in the mass of faces, we'd share a nod.

During SOI we learned basic war-fighting tactics such as squad rushes, claymore emplacement, digging fighting holes, and land navigation. During squad rushes, we were given a magazine of live ammunition and put in a field facing rows of automated plastic silhouettes of people. We were split into groups of 13 or so and told to bound towards the targets. During bounding, half of us would shoot at the targets while the other six or seven would run forward.

While we ran, we said to ourselves, "I'm up. He sees me. I'm down." The idea behind this ditty was to get up when one says "I'm up.," run during "He sees me," and lastly, hit the deck when one says, "I'm down." This technique is supposed to prevent an enemy from having enough time to aim and fire.

During the rushes, as we ran, dove and fired past each other, the 0331s were training on their machine guns. They sat on a hill shooting over our heads at another set of targets on a hill perpendicular to us. On top of our own rounds whizzing through the air and the crack of the bullets hitting the targets, we also had machine guns firing at targets to our left!

During other phases, they let each student throw a live grenade. Two students were picked to fire the AT-4 rocket launcher, and the instructors set off a claymore at a group of watermelons to show us the damage it would do.

We spent several days sleeping in chest deep holes we dug in the woods, protecting ourselves from the other platoon as they patrolled to find and attack us. Sometimes we patrolled with lasers attached to our rifles and receptors on our helmets and flak jackets. When we fired the blanks (ammunition with no bullets) at each other, the lasers would register the recoil of the rifle and shoot at whatever we were aiming. The receptors on our helmets and gear would register a laser hit and glow red if we had been shot.

Three times we went on ruck marches and each needed to be passed in order to proceed with training. The longest was 20 km (or clicks) with full pack and weapons. The mortar teams had to carry their incredibly heavy mortar tubes while the machine gunners had to carry their heavy machine guns. I did not envy them.

During each part of training, I was absorbing as much information as possible. There was competition between each of the infantry MOSs on ruck marches and during PT. But for those of us entering into Recon training, we knew we had more hurt ahead of us.

Of the 250 or so in SOI, around 50 had been eligible to listen to the briefing. Of those 50, 22 had tried out at the pool. Of the 22 who went, seven of us passed the Recon screening; Steshko, Diener, Bailey, D'Errico, Bonopartis, Kaliszewski, and myself.

There was another Marine from the fleet (Evans) who had also passed making us eight on the day of the screening. After SOI graduation, a van would pick us up and take us to the next step: Recon Training Platoon or RTP.

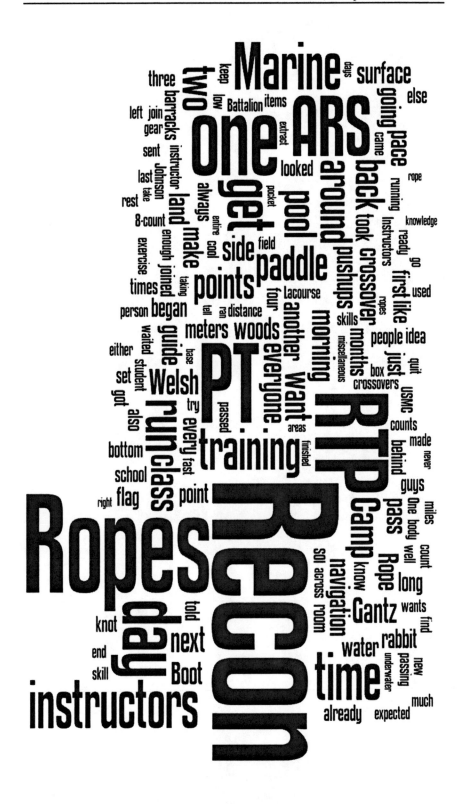

Teaching The Ropes

SOI came and went. I had graduated Boot Camp on August 10th, three months after I entered the USMC. I entered into SOI ten days later and graduated on October 8th, 2004.

When graduation day arrived, all our bags were packed and staged outside. The other Marines in our class had already been told what unit they were going to and each group of Marines was arranged according to final destination. I could see the 1st Battalion, 9th Marines or 1/9 over in one area, and the mortar school Marines over in another. Large groups of guys exchanged emails and phone numbers as they waited for the buses to take them to their next set of racks. My time in the USMC so far had been one set of squad bays followed by another; one set of instructors replaced by the other.

The seven of us who had passed the Recon test already knew each others' names and we waited off to the side. Gantz was also with us, given a reprieve for his attitude. D'Errico and Bailey were two of my closest friends. D'Errico and I had met Josiah Bailey in SOI. True to the Recon nature, Bailey had achieved almost every single honor and award that one can receive in Boot Camp: guide, honor guide, and ironman. He was an incredibly strong and fast Marine who prided himself on his Christian faith.

As we waited, a van pulled up to take us to the Recon barracks. We didn't recognize or know the driver at all. He was a redhead who didn't say much to us. We had no idea if he was a Recon Marine or a POG (Person Other than Grunt) so we hoisted our bags into the van and got in. We didn't even know where we were going.

Camp Geiger, where SOI and MCT are held, is just a few miles from Camp Lejeune, the 2nd Marine Division base. As we drove over the bridge into the back gate of Camp Lejeune, we saw a helicopter (helo) flying low over the river. Attached to the bottom of the helo by a thick rope were five guys hanging from harnesses.

"Who can tell me what those guys are doing?" the driver queried us.

"They're SPIE rigging," Steshko said. "I love military history books, and I read all about Recon."

Diener looked around at us. "Maybe it's an omen. Eight of us are being driven to Recon training. Perhaps only five will make it through."

Recon Training Platoon is a stepping stone to the Amphibious Reconnaissance School or ARS. ARS is where one is awarded the MOS of 0321 and title of Recon Marine. RTP is where one gets the training to pass. ARS is a tough, grueling school which, contrary to Boot Camp, is more physically than mentally demanding. On the west coast, Marines in RTP go through the Basic Reconnaissance Course or BRC. I have no idea what BRC entails but it's identical in information, if not in format. Nowadays all Recon Marines train at BRC on the west coast. ARS no longer exists.

During RTP, I was given a rope which I wore as a sash around my body signifying the training status and illegitimacy around the battalion, much like the glow belt at Boot Camp. Because of this sash, RTP Marines are called "Ropes". All the other Recon Marines treat Ropes like crap and Ropes avoid the gaze, attention, and scorn of the Recon Marines as best as they can. Much like Boot Camp, Marines in RTP are at the bottom of the totem pole. When a Recon Marine walks through the hallways of the office building, Ropes are expected to jump aside and let him pass.

The purpose behind RTP is to get Marines ready to pass ARS. RTP involves lots of intense PT and studying knowledge in a variety of areas. From sun up to sun down (and usually beyond these times), Ropes are learning skills and doing 8-count body-builders to pass the time.

An 8-count body-builder is a favorite exercise to punish or discipline Recon Marines. Starting at the position of attention, the Marine squats and shoots his legs out behind him to end up in the pushup position. Two counts have already been accomplished. Next, a simple pushup is done followed by spreading the legs apart, and bringing them back together. These steps make up another four counts, bringing the total to six. Lastly, the feet are brought back to the hands, putting the Marine in a squat, and then finally standing up finishing the last two counts of the exercise. This entire sequence counts as one 8-count body-builder. Marines in Recon usually do this for hours. For embarrassing a team leader (TL) or missing a deadline, a Rope or Recon Marine can expect at least 500 8-counts.

Besides PT all day, every day, Ropes are used to police call (clean) the barracks, organize miscellaneous areas, and perform any necessary duty that the base might require of Recon Battalion. They do the dirty work that no one else wants to do. For example, if the base commander wants 50 Marines from each battalion to attend a briefing about morale and haircuts, the Ropes will be the ones sent to the briefing.

We pulled into the barracks at Courthouse Bay and checked into our rooms, aided by a few Ropes that were already in RTP. Ropes are constantly being circulated into ARS. Marines in RTP continued to train until an ARS school slot opened up. Sometimes that was four months after he joined; sometimes he got lucky and headed to ARS within two weeks.

The barracks were a large, impersonal, three-story brick building (much like a motel) with catwalks around the outside joining the rooms to one another. The regular Recon Marines stay in the same barracks and are grouped by platoon and company. The Ropes' rooms were on the third floor as far as possible from everyone else; out of sight – out of mind.

We stayed two to a room. The Marine I was staying with was a guy named Clement. He would leave for an ARS class before me, drop out, and be sent to Light Armored Reconnaissance Battalion (LAR). Within a year of joining LAR, he would be killed in Iraq.

As I dumped my stuff on my side of the room, I turned to the tasks appointed to me upon arriving at Recon. It was Friday and we were told to memorize the Recon Creed and get our PT gear ready for Monday morning.

Recon is a volunteer MOS. One doesn't accidentally wind up in Recon and therefore the Recon community wants only the best and brightest of those who really want to be there. Traditionally, the first day of RTP is a grueling day of intense PT with runs, swamp swims, and log PT in order to weed out those who join without any idea of what they are doing and lacking motivation. I was ignorant of what Recon was like, but I didn't know how to quit.

Monday morning arrived and we joined the other Ropes down by the car park. The 13 of us were in shirts, shorts, and sneakers. A few other Ropes were nursing injuries which was common at the time for RTP.

The Recon Instructors showed up and we realized they were the same ones from the screening. They introduced themselves as Sgt Aldana, Cpl Welsh, and SSgt Johnson. The three of them gave us a quick low down of what to expect from RTP and told us to keep our noses clean and out of trouble. We would have to learn how to do things on the fly because there was no lesson book for RTP. We briefly stretched out and then darted off towards the trees across the road.

Most Recon runs are done with a rabbit. The rabbit is a fast runner who sets the pace for everyone else. If it's a graded run, one has to finish with the rabbit or lose points. Lose enough points and one fails the run. The amount of points for each minute behind the rabbit changes based on the distance of the run. If the run is conducted for general PT and not scored, Marines will get chided for not finishing well with the result of extra PT for not keeping up. Extra PT is never fun and provides enough motivation to run as fast as possible to keep up with the rabbit. There was no such thing as an "easy day".

Aldana led on the first day and took off at a break-neck pace. Being new Ropes, the eight of us tried to keep up as he neared the trees a few hundred yards away. The other Ropes warned us as we passed to save our strength because the pace was just going to get faster. We also had no idea how long the run was going to last. We foolishly didn't listen and as soon as Aldana hit the trail through the woods, he began sprinting, leaving us behind.

The trail wove through the trees for two miles before we broke out onto a tank trail. Running at a dead sprint, I was only barely able to keep up. As the distance on the run increased, we began to fall out. I had no idea how long the run was supposed to go on for, but with Recon Instructors assessing our willingness, giving up wasn't an option. After all, maybe just around the next bend was the finish line.

That PT lasted for nine miles. Every couple of miles we stopped to do pushups, 8-count body builders, or some other form of calisthenics. At one point in the run, we belly-crawled through a thick, marshy bog. As we crawled in line, people began to throw up from the swamp smell and exhaustion. The rest of us had to wade through the vomit. Even Welsh, leading at this point, puked from the smell. Regardless of what they asked of me, or what conditions I found myself in, I just kept running.

I finished that run well and as we finished, we circled up to stretch and wait for stragglers. Welsh came running up with Gantz.

"Everybody listen up. Gantz has something he wants to tell you," Welsh said. We walked in a circle to cool down and looked over at Gantz, not sure what was going on. Gantz stood at parade rest, not saying a word.

"Go on," Welsh goaded. "Tell them what you told me." Gantz mumbled something quietly.

"Louder," Welsh demanded.

"I said 'I quit'," Gantz repeated, louder this time. Johnson, who was in charge of the training in RTP, burst out laughing.

"Oh! Ha! Good. Well, that's exactly what we want," Johnson said. Quitting is as repulsive to a Recon Marine as vomiting into holy water is to a Catholic priest.

The rest of that day was pushups, pull-ups, and other forms of PT. I looked over during pushups at another Rope who had been there a few months. With my arms drained and giving out, Welsh asked me to quit, incredulous at my weakness, trying to get me to give up.

"Is it Vandekar? Give up, Vandekar. Are you serious? You don't want to be here either. Look at you! You can't even do a pushup. Just join Gantz and be a quitter," Welsh taunted.

The Rope next to me with stark red hair, a Marine named Steve Barker, looked over and said, "I fucking love this shit!"

Ropes learn a traditional set of pushups called 25 & 5. This exercise is a set of 25 pushups with a pause before the next 5. During these last 5 pushups we yell "Want to be" each time, finishing with "RECON" ("Want to be, want to be, want to be, want to be, want to be Recon!"). After passing Recon training, the exercise yell changes to "Airborne, diver, Recon, ranger, Valhalla!"

The instructors of RTP came up with creative ways to wear us out for PT; carry a brick underwater across the bottom of the deep end while fighting off other Ropes trying to get it back to their side was known as underwater hockey; bear crawl on all fours across a football field with the winner excused from the next lap. The winners of some exercises were rewarded with a reprieve from the next lap or mile of PT. This incentive ensured that we ran or swam as fast as we could to sit out the rest of the torture. "It pays to be a winner," the instructors yelled from the side.

Over the course of training for ARS, we got thrashed with intense PT every morning. At some point, each RTP session contains a week at the pool as well. We swam endless back-to-back crossovers as well as thousands of meters for time; all in full camis and sometimes with boots. The pool is the worst part of RTP.

The knowledge at RTP was taught to ensure the Ropes will have an advantage at ARS, being familiar with the knowledge. The endless PT was to help get Ropes ready for day two of ARS. Day two was a bone-crushing weeding out session that the ARS instructors used to make people quit. All day PT was expected on day two with an incredibly high drop-out rate.

One particular long day in the pool, the instructors decided to end with crossovers. We all gathered on the side of the pool in the water, waiting for the signal.

"Prepare to crossover," yelled the instructor. All eyes shifted from the instructor to the other side of the pool, focusing on our goal and taking slow, steady breaths.

"Prepare to crossover," we repeated.

"Crossover!" yelled the instructor.

"Crossover!" we chorused back. Some students didn't bother yelling. After the command, we immediately began swimming for the other side of the pool. Any hesitation meant extra PT so everyone left simultaneously.

As we left the surface, all of us headed for the bottom. Crossovers were easier if one wasn't tempted to get air just a few feet above. We kept our eyes focused on the bottom of the pool and not on the wall in front of us. If I looked up, my mind would begin to tell me that I had only enough air to make it. If I didn't know how much I had left to swim, I could hold my breath longer.

When I reached the opposite side, I headed to the surface with my fist above my head; a technique used to clear debris were this a real life scenario. On the surface, we tried to breathe calmly and deeply as we knew we would only get three breaths before we heard, "Prepare to crossover!"

The first twelve crossovers were largely successful before people started to come to the surface early with lack of air. Instructors swam across the surface without camis. They glided smoothly through the water, watching us with goggles or masks on. Any student who started to come up either got attacked on the surface or pushed immediately under again.

By the 18th crossover they incited the familiar winner's mantra and suddenly people who came to the surface every time, managed to stay under for an additional crossover. Each time the crossover ended, the instructors would pull out the fastest swimmer. The instructors were motivating us to find the stamina to do one more even when we thought we couldn't. I counted 32 crossovers till the last of us got out.

On another day at the pool, the instructors said that if we could swim the entire 50 meters underwater on the first try, we would be allowed to skip today's pool PT. Three out of every four Ropes miraculously made it the entire length. If you had asked us to do a 50 meter crossover with no incentive, no one would've passed.

One of the important lessons ground into me during RTP, was the lesson about panic. The DIs at Boot Camp always assured us that we were going to Iraq and gave us the mentality that we could kill, but the Recon instructors took a different approach. They showed us through thrashing, drowning, and making us uncomfortable in the woods or water, that a situation could get beyond our control. It was during these moments that they assured us we had to remain cool and not panic. Panic, they said, was when the body stopped the natural instinct for survival. A panicking person could fight off a rescuer, struggle vainly against ropes, or make irrational decisions to endanger themselves and others.

Every couple of weeks, new Ropes would join our class. I had joined RTP in October, 2004. Another ARS class started in November but only the senior Ropes were sent. Some people were dropped from ARS and were sent back to retrain in RTP and attend the next class. Joe Lacourse was one of these Marines.

As I was running from my room to PT one morning in late October, I ran around a corner and smacked right into Lacourse. He was a 6′ 2″ Marine from Massachusetts with a short fuse for mundane tasks or things he felt hindered his ability to operate. Recon was his life; he lived and breathed the Recon creed.

He was checking into his new room when we smacked into each other. New Ropes normally respected the guys who had been there earlier and without knowing he was actually senior to me, I expected this Marine to move aside and let me pass.

"How about you get the fuck out of my way?!" Lacourse demanded. Already on a timeline, I stepped aside and ran down to the others. As I passed, he pantomimed strangling me and clenched his teeth in frustration.

"What the hell is that guy's problem?" I wondered. Lacourse

would have to repeat everything at RTP and ARS in order to try out for Recon again. He was understandably pissed despite his short temper.

We never doubted our instructors' ability or stamina. One morning, Johnson took us out to the PT field and said we could all be excused from PT that day if one of us could copy him. He proceeded to do a one-legged squat on each leg, flawlessly. We fell over in our attempts and soon after, the running commenced.

Each morning, the rabbit would run a certain distance and make it back to the flag pole by 0800 where the engineer school would raise the flag for morning Colors. If we were too slow and didn't make it to the flag pole by the time the engineers began Colors, it was akin to missing extraction with a helicopter. The late-comers would have to extend the run simulating the movement back to friendly lines. You didn't want to be one of the guys who missed extract.

Metaphors like this one were used continuously in our training and especially in our PT. If a run did not finish in time, we would have to escape and evade (E&E). Other mornings we would low crawl through sand and water and other muck in order to learn the workings of natural camouflage or maintaining a low profile. We were constantly learning and picking up skills to get ready for ARS.

Besides PT in the morning, we also spent the day learning land navigation, knot tying, and radio procedures amongst other skills. We learned a skill first in a classroom setting with hands on exercises from the instructors and then took it into the field to try it for real as practical application.

We always had our ropes around our bodies and our rubber rifles one-arm's distance away. We were also told to have several pocket items at all times including note taking gear (pen and paper), protractor, map, compass, knife, and a few other miscellaneous items. We did everything (except land navigation) in pairs. "Two is one – one is none" was a common expression harping on the importance of redundancy.

Before land navigation began, we always refreshed our pace count. A pace count is the number of right-footed steps (or left-footed) it takes a person to travel 100 meters. The pace count changes due to terrain, elevation, and gear. Mine was 72 at the time. A person walking uphill will have a larger number of paces than one walking downhill. Just as easily, a person wearing a rifle on his right shoulder will veer to the right. Being off by only one degree for 1,000 meters means a Marine will be standing 17 meters away from where he intended. 17 meters is large enough not to see a green box in the woods.

Land navigation was conducted over several days on several courses including the USMC sniper school course. We were given a compass and 10 points. We plotted the points with a terrain map and protractor and found our azimuths from terrain elevation or landmarks. We took off with our rubber rifles, canteens, and the typical RTP pocket items and scoured the woods for green boxes with spray painted numbers. We were forbidden to use roads or talk to other Ropes we met on the course.

Due to pace count inaccuracies and the inability to walk in a straight line through the woods, it was always interesting to stop at a place where I expected a box to be and look around to find nothing. Which way should I go to begin looking for my point? Is it ahead or behind? A Rope can quickly get lost by wandering in circles, looking for a point.

For this reason, it was important to remember the three rules of Recon:

1. Always look cool
2. Always know where you are
3. If you get lost, try to look cool

During the day, instructors drove up and down the roads trying to catch us taking the easy route and walking on the roads. At the end of the day we returned by the deadline (extract) to find Ropes doing pushups or digging graves. These Ropes had been caught on the road. Because they were caught, it could also mean that everyone else was going to join them if the instructors were in a bad mood. Other infractions included losing any of one's pocket items, failing to find all the required points, or returning to the starting point late (missing extract).

After each day of land navigation the instructors would check our points. The points were brown or green boxes in the middle of the woods with letter-number combinations. Once we found the box we were looking for, we wrote down the number on the box. After a few days, the Ropes in my class banded together and decided to help each other out.

"Guys, there's no reason we can't all pass land nav and save ourselves a little grief and stress. We'll meet up at 450321 130321. Bring your points from yesterday and we'll swap answers," said Brink, a senior Rope to me. "If you really want some practice, do the points on your own, but don't dime out anyone else."

That day in the woods we shared stories, joked and felt good about passing. About an hour before we had to return, we split up and went our separate ways to return to the start from different directions and at different times. We finished the day with everyone passing land navigation and everyone made it back on time.

Knot tying was a skill picked up through repetition. There was not a lot of punishment involved with failure since simply tying the same knot repeatedly would exponentially increase the skill. Most of the time we would just have to continually tie it until everyone was up to speed and within regulations.

There were roughly 13 knots, each with their own corresponding time to complete it, ranging from thirty seconds to two minutes depending on the complexity of the knot. The remainder of the rope after the knot was tied was called a pigtail and, when held in the hand, had to be longer than one's fist yet shorter than a fist and thumb. Essentially, the room for error was the length of one's thumb.

As we always had our ropes on us tied in a sash around our body, we could practice our knot-tying when standing around waiting for instructors or after chow. Once we made Recon, these knots enabled us to lash things down in zodiac rafts (small rubber boats) or secure our rifles and our gear with dummy cords.

Another Rope tradition, and a tradition in many areas of the military, involves the unit flag, or guidon. A guidon is a small flag that is custom made to represent a platoon or squad. In Boot Camp, each platoon and company had a guidon. This flag embodies a unit and in RTP, it is represented by a paddle. There is a lot of tradition in the Recon paddle but that'll be discussed later.

At all times during any training, and with few exceptions, the instructors attempted to steal our paddle while we guarded it from them. The paddle is safe by itself during pool PT when everyone is in the water, and perhaps one or two other instances. But during chow, sleeping at night, on field exercises, and during PT the paddle accompanied the Ropes. The lead student, known as the guide, was responsible for carrying it, however he could hand it off if he needed to use both hands for a task.

Instructors slyly shimmied over to the paddle to grab it and run, or simply attacked the guide to take it from him. Typically it was tied around and to the guide by parachute cord known as 550 cord. But in the case of a theft, every student abandoned training and protocol to get it back. Physical abuse of an instructor was never tolerated and severely punished except in this case.

Often times, if regular Recon Marines unassociated with Rope training saw the paddle blatantly unguarded, they took it. It was not long after that, that a fight broke out between Ropes and Recon Marines in a desperate attempt to retrieve the paddle.

If the Recon Marines succeeded in keeping the paddle, it proved that the Ropes were unworthy of passing training and unless the Commandant of the USMC himself was there, they would thrash long into the night with hard PT and dig countless graves for themselves. Also, the paddle would probably get broken, repainted with rainbows and flowers, or marked through some other form of disrespect.

If the Ropes succeeded in retrieving the paddle, they reestablished their honor but would likely thrash as punishment for losing it in the first place. At the very least, the guide would be fired and a new student will become guide.

After a training session of a few months, with a pool week, land navigation, knot work, radios, and other miscellaneous skills, an ARS class opened up. The top students were picked to go, either by seniority or skill.

I joined RTP three or four weeks before a class picked up and waited about four months for the next class to begin. On January 23rd, I left for ARS and joined a class of Marines testing for Force Recon and Recon Battalion. There were about sixty of us at the beginning, with Marines from the fleet, Ropes with only a week of training, and Marines who had already attempted to pass another time before. I would either leave in two and half months with the coveted title of "Recon Marine", or in shame long before that.

Oh, Three, Twenty-One

Those of us who were given an ARS school slot carpooled from Camp Lejeune, North Carolina to Fort Story, Virginia in our civilian vehicles. It was January 23rd, 2005 – a Sunday. Fort Story is a very small reserve Army base near Norfolk and most times is nearly deserted. Just inside the fort gate was a fenced in compound which housed the Amphibious Reconnaissance School (ARS).

We pulled into the base and parked our cars outside the fence in a line. As we stood looking up the hill over the PT table and pull-up bars, we heard the waves on the other side of the hill crashing on the beach. It was cold, and as we nervously stood there, it began to snow. There's a common expression in the military that goes, "if it ain't raining, we ain't training." This saying is especially true of snow, but it doesn't rhyme. While we huddled in our jackets and watched the snow come down, we knew it was going to be a miserable set of months ahead.

The compound consisted of a few one-story tan buildings. The first one closest to the road was the classroom and offices for the ARS instructors (commonly called cadre). So far, our DIs had been the scariest Marines we had come across. Our SOI instructors had treated us firmly, but with care and while the RTP instructors thrashed us at all hours, they had their moments when they sympathized with us. After all, we were (hopefully) soon going to return as Recon Marines. However, the cadre were a completely different breed.

We had only heard of them in stories but we knew they were not there to mess around. They treated us honestly and fairly but they were there to uphold the Recon standards. They would weed out the weak and wounded. If anyone was not ready for ARS, the training continued anyway. The cadre were there to ensure that we put one foot in front of the other, or got out of the way. They never watched from the side as we PT-ed, but got in the sand with us and outperformed us on every task. They were legends.

The building closest to the classrooms was the barracks with two wings of bunkbeds and a common room connecting them. The barracks also had communal showers. As we entered the building a white board stood on an easel with a promise inscribed by the cadre: "Only the strong will stay."

The other buildings consisted of the Battalion Aid Station (BAS), a boat locker, and a supply room. These meager buildings sitting at the bottom of a small hill, walled off by chain link fence from the outside world, gave off a very unfamiliar and chilling feeling as the snow came down.

We had arrived on a Sunday and the instructor who checked us in let us know that we would start bright and early on Monday with a traditional Recon Screening. The screening would ascertain who wanted to be there and who had slipped through the cracks. "Be ready for day two" were his parting words.

To start Monday, we ran a PFT to weed out those who were not ready. It was your typical three mile run, with pull-ups and crunches for a total score of 300. All of us had to get a first class PFT (over 225) in order to remain in the class. We then bussed to the pool on a nearby Navy base to perform the swim section of the screening as mentioned in the previous chapters.

By this stage in training, I could do a crossover in my sleep and tread water for hours without any sign of panic. When we began the confined tread, those of us from RTP had a technique. We no longer panicked or resisted going underwater. The screening was mostly for the fleet Marines who were unprepared and had not gone through RTP.

ARS consisted of a lot of what we had been trying to get a grasp of in RTP; knot work, land navigation, patrolling, swimming, radios, and of course, lots of intense PT. All the lessons were a little more structured and everything was now graded. Not only did we have to keep up with the PT and exercises, we had to pass the academic tests, tie your knots correctly, and navigate to your points in order to remain in the school. Failure to meet any of these requirements on any day meant a quick ticket home, not another chance or a couple hundred 8-count body builders.

On the second day of ARS, they brought out the big guns to scare any volunteers who didn't have the heart. This PT was RTP style, full of log runs and no end calisthenics. The cadre ran us up and down sandy hills and forced us to carry logs in endless circles just to see who would drop. They were looking to break us and it continued all day. The people who quit found their name on a stick covered in animal skulls called the bone pole. Over the course of the school, more names joined the bone pole as people gave up, failed academically, or weren't able to keep up with the PT.

Every Friday we went on a ruck run. Rucks refer to a large backpack, much like civilians carry for camping, but without all the bling and color. Each Thursday we'd be given the assigned weight to pack in the ruck, whether it was 35 lbs or 50 lbs.

Typically we started at smaller weights on smaller runs ranging from three to five miles. As the weight increased, so did the distance. The base was only a few miles wide so this meant we had to run past the compound several times. Every run ended at the compound so it created an illusion of a finish line every time we ran by.

We didn't know how long the run was going to be so the illusion generated what we called the mind-fuck. Essentially, one's mind started to give up if it thought the end was near even though one had strength remaining. This concept was true on a long run or a crossover. One just had to power through it and realize it was all in the head and run past the illusion of a finish line.

Every run started very early in the morning, and because we were a winter class, we stood out in the cold in t-shirts and cami bottoms cinching down the straps on our rucks. We only wore t-shirts because before we had run one mile, we would be sweating from the exertion. Bailey and several others got hypothermia on one run as the sweat froze to their faces.

Each ruck had to be weighed before the run and before water was added by the cadre. If a ruck weighed under the prescribed weight, the Marine would still have to run but with a sandbag given by an instructor. Undoubtedly, the instructor sandbags were way over the weight limit. Because we never wanted to suffer anymore than we had to, sandbags always weighed at least five pounds heavier to avoid any discrepancy.

On top of the sandbags, we had to carry camelbacks strapped to the top for hydration. So the water we brought was an increase to the weight. We also carried four canteens of water, a rifle, and two ammo pouches, while running in our cami bottoms and boots. The sandbag (55-60 lbs), ruck (2.5 lbs), camelback (6-8 lbs), canteens (8 lbs), magazines (1 lb), one chow (1 lb), our rubber rifle (8 lbs), poncho and poncho liner (3 lbs), and 782-gear to carry the pouches (3 lbs) all added up to about 88 lbs conservatively, not including our boots and camis.

The cadre showed up, equally burdened with rucks, some with safety equipment, and one on an ATV. They had radios and tested their gear to ensure we were safe. Chemlights were dropped during the run because the sun woke up after we did. Inevitably we would get strung out during the run and have to follow the trail of chemlights as we searched for the rabbit.

After weighing the rucks, we lined up outside the ARS compound and waited for the start. The rabbit instructor would take off without warning and the beginning was always the same; the rabbit would hit the beach and run in the softest sand for a mile or two before heading inland to the trails amongst the trees.

Another inevitable part of the run was what we called Lochness. It was a sandy, almost vertical hill. Sometimes the run consisted of several trips up Lochness, with an instructor giving us a rubber band on each trip to ensure honesty. No one wanted to go up Lochness any more than necessary.

The trail up Lochness was wide enough for only one person at a time. Because the trail was loose sand, it was crucial to establish footholds by digging our boots in. The cadre would watch to make sure we powered up it without using our hands for support on the ground or by grabbing a tree. If someone who was fatigued got to Lochness before you, he'd crush all the footholds already made in the loose sand. Getting to Lochness ahead of others was the key.

As I ran, blindly following a trail of lights, cadre would run past with hands in pockets as if they did this everyday. Some of them did. If a student didn't pass the ruck run, he wouldn't get any liberty that weekend and a Marine could only fail two ruck runs before he failed PT for the course. So I put my head down and ran as fast as my body let me and hoped to get back in time to pass. Each run also counted towards our graduating score.

To me, it seemed unfair that a 200 lb Marine was asked to carry the same weight as a 150 lb Marine. But in the end, I reasoned that I was tougher than guys bigger than me as I was being asked to carry a larger percentage of my weight.

There were other PT sessions involving log runs, a full day up and down Lochness, calisthenics around the PT table, and of course plenty of regular runs in shorts and t-shirts at a much faster pace.

We learned how to do military sketches and were given homework to sketch out a building on the base using the techniques we had mastered. We learned how to call in air support and med-evac wounded Marines using field radios. We learned to assemble terrain models of the compound using sand and common items. We took memory games and academic tests, all of which we had to pass in order to continue onto the next task. Each evening we'd recoup, straighten up our gear, and get ourselves ready for the next day.

A lot of these skills and games required an intense concentration to detail. We would be asked to recall how many shower heads were in the bathroom or how many lights were on the ceiling. Or we'd watch a clip of a movie before a class then have to recall what car models were in the clip. They were always asking and pushing us to notice the little things during every part of our day which forced us to be aware of our surroundings.

For chow, we'd be driven by bus to the chow hall. However, the bus would stop a few hundred meters from the chow hall and we'd pair up to carry each other the rest of the way. On the way out, we'd have to pair up again and run back to the bus with the other person carrying; just another way to make something ordinarily enjoyable completely miserable. But it all served a purpose, in this case mastering a wounded-man carry.

For the first stage of land navigation, we practiced on a small course on the base at Fort Story. The course consisted of two rows of ten boxes facing each other across a few hundred meters of woods. We started on one row and were given coordinates to a box in the opposite row to practice our pace count and dead-reckoning. The boxes in each row were only a few yards apart from each other, so we had to be as accurate as possible or we'd end up at the box next to the correct one.

For the land navigation test, we drove a few hours to AP Hill, a base farther north in Virginia. AP Hill was a much larger, professional course. We were situated in a set of squad bays for a few days while we were tested on land navigation.

It was at the beginning of land navigation that a young Marine named Keith Zeier developed a problem with his ankle. Over the course of PT, his Achilles tendon had begun separating from his ankle, causing him excruciating pain. Zeier had been in RTP before me and had joined the USMC when a friend's father, who was a firefighter, had been killed in the World Trade Center attacks.

Zeier wanted to be Recon so badly he had kept running, often finishing among the top five despite the immense pain in his ankle. The corpsman in charge of ARS had told Zeier that if he continued running, he might limp the rest of his life. Zeier refused to quit and at land navigation, the swelling was getting unbearable.

Knowing Zeier was a Christian, I called Bailey and D'Errico over to pray over his ankle. We told Zeier that if he believed it, God would give it to him.

Much like the training at RTP, we were given ten navigation points to find during the day and five at night. There were orienteering punches instead of numbers at the points. When we approached a sign, we punched a card with the orienteering punch and continued on to the next point.

Just like in RTP we were not allowed to use roads. We were also not allowed to help other students we saw on the way. We had to secure eight out of the ten during the day and four out of the five at night in order to pass. We were given just enough time that forced us to jog the entire distance and couldn't dilly dally looking blindly for a sign.

Each punch was unique so there was no way to share answers and cheat. Meeting up at a random location in the woods wasn't going to help anyone. However, there was snow on the ground so when I headed towards the last four or five points, I simply followed the footprints in the snow. Some of the footprints veered off in random directions but the closer I was to the sign, the closer the footprints converged on each other. By studying the footprints on the ground, I could roughly guess which way the sign lay.

Once I reached the sign, I softly tapped my pen on the metal so that if there was another student nearby in the woods, he would hear the little ping. That sound was unmistakable amongst the muffled sounds of a winter wood.

The first day at AP Hill was the first chance to pass. As I jogged through the woods to my first point, I checked my watch for the time. I was surprised to realize that it was my 20th birthday! "I must save a little pound cake from my MRE [Meal Ready-to-Eat]," I thought to myself.

That evening we tried the night course. It was the same course with fewer points. We were not permitted to use white light to search for our points in addition to all the same rules.

The end of Patrol Week, at the start of the run

A terrain model made by the class out of sand

I secured my first four points at night without a problem but struggled to find my fifth point. After wandering in circles for several minutes, I decided I needed to head back towards the start in order to make it on time without losing any points for lateness. When I got there, I realized I had misjudged the distance and was 45 minutes early. We were not permitted to check in early if we hadn't gotten all of our points, so I curled up in the snow a few hundred yards away in the woods.

We had infrared strobes so the cadre could see us with night vision as they searched the woods. I concealed the strobe in my gear, set my alarm on my watch and tucked it underneath my beanie. I placed it next to my ear so I would be sure it woke me up, and stole some illegal Z's. When the alarm went off, I gathered my gear, replaced the strobe, and jogged to the finish looking worn out and exhausted.

Those who didn't pass the initial day and night course were given another try the next day and night. Those of us who passed both courses successfully the first time took a quick and fun survival course. The cadre taught us how to make shelter in the woods, fashion traps and tools out of sticks, and catch and purify water. They even had live chickens to kill, skin, and cook.

There were other events at ARS that I thought were fun and interesting to learn. Stalking was one of the most difficult skills to master. The cadre put us at one end of a 200 meter field with low shrubbery and brush. There were no ditches or hills to hide behind except for a slight curve which hid the starting line from the finish.

We were instructed to camouflage our gear with natural vegetation and crawl from one end to the other. At the finish line were an instructor with binoculars and a radio sitting on a HMMWV (High Mobility Multiple Wheeled Vehicle or hummvee). He was calling out directions to cadre in the field to walk onto our positions. The instructors in the field would only "catch" a student if the instructor had been walked directly on top of him.

As I began my creep, I slowly pushed down tall blades of grass. I had been in an event like this during RTP when RTP instructors had failed to see me lying in bushes next to them. I learned patience and the necessity to move slowly.

During the creep, a walking instructor began to move toward me from the directions on the walkie-talkie. I lay perfectly still. I didn't put my head down, or close my eyes or make any movement. Any slight attempt to hide may actually betray my position. The instructor

The dreaded Lochness trail through the trees

Lining up for the last run of ARS on graduation day

walked over me and stopped a few paces away. I could hear the "enemy" at the other end trying to find me. The instructor stood a few feet away and the walkie-talkie blurted, "Sniper at your feet."

"Nope. There is no one here," was the response from the instructor in the field. The "enemy" continued scanning for other students. After all, there were 50 more of us trying to get him. I remained motionless for several minutes before considering it safe to continue my progress.

I almost made it to the very end by inching my way slowly through grass and brush. It was a game of patience and just 15 meters from the rope signaling the finish line, the instructor caught sight of me. One of my canteen snaps had flashed in the sunlight. Though it was a fun exercise to practice, no student made it to the finish unseen.

During ARS, the students were split up into five to eight man teams and given a team leader within the group. An instructor also paired up with us to help with any difficult subjects, assess our progress, and steer us in the right direction. My instructor was a Marine named Sergeant Guendner who had taught at the school for three years. He was a huge hulk of a Marine who took pride when his team succeeded, and punished us when we failed.

Over the course of the school, my team was made up of two Marines from the reserves, two guys who had tried to pass before from the fleet and three RTP Marines who came in with me: Barker, D'Errico, and Lacourse. We had a sergeant, three corporals, three lance corporals, and me, Private First Class (the second to lowest rank in the USMC) Vandekar, the most junior member of the team.

During one PT exercise, the team leader (TL) for my team had come out without a shave. Guendner pulled him aside after PT and calling the team together, appointed me TL. We had already switched TLs two or three times so I think Guendner appointed me (the most junior in rank and physically smallest) initially to make a point. However, I remained the TL for the rest of ARS.

All the Marines who graduated with passing scores received the MOS 0321, though some were testing to join Force Recon and others, like me, were joining Recon Battalion. Surprisingly, during my school the battalion guys were doing better in all areas than the Force guys. I had two Force wannabes in my team who never passed.

Force Recon Company was the unit one step up from Reconnaissance Battalion. Force took Recon Marines who had survived one or two deployments and offered them a position in a Force Recon team if they had a good reputation and enough time in their enlistment. However, they attended the same school (ARS/BRC) and held the same MOS (0321).

ARS culminated in a grueling ordeal that we call Patrol Week. Utilizing everything we learned in school, we participated in six simulated missions rotating as a different position in the team each night; Team Leader (TL), Assistant Team Leader (ATL), Radio Transmission Operator (RTO), Assistant Radio Transmission Operator (ARTO), Pointman, and Slackman.

The TL was ultimately responsible for everything the team does or fails to do. He was usually second in the lineup in a ranger file, behind the Pointman and after the RTO.

A ranger file is simply patrolling in a single file line. This formation has the advantage of reducing a team's trail if they were being followed. An enemy may know from the trail where they've been, but won't know how many. This formation is also used for dense vegetation so that the first two or three members break the shrubbery and the remaining team members follow in their path.

The Pointman walked in front of the TL, navigating to the destination. The Pointman and the TL knew where the team was at all times (Recon rule #2). The ATL brought up the rear of the formation, checking for anything that was dropped at each location that the team stopped. The RTO and ARTO handled communications. The RTO usually followed the TL to provide him with the radio in case of emergency. The Slackman carried any extra gear and also served as the team machine gunner.

As the TL for the team during the school, I started off as TL on the first patrol. There were six unique missions involving Observation Posts (O.P.s) on Prisoner Of War (POW) camps, a bridge report, a military sketch of a compound, and other skills we had acquired over the school phase.

During Patrol Week, we were allowed two patrols under 80 percent. The patrols were graded on our leadership, billet responsibilities, situational awareness, and mission accomplishment. After the second grade under 80 percent, a Marine would get counseled and if he received a third, he failed the school.

During the day, my team was separated a short distance from the other teams in a cleared out section of the woods back at AP Hill called the harbor site. In the morning, the instructor who would be grading our next patrol came over and gave us our mission and requirements. During the day we planned out our mission for the next evening. Even though we could see the other teams, none of the teams shared information or spoke to each other.

After the instructor gave us the quick brief on where we were going and for what purpose, the TL had ten minutes to prepare a warning order complete with gear load-out, food and water rations, and any special needs he thought were necessary. In a few hours, we issued an operation order complete with a full terrain model, the route we would patrol, and details for actions on the objective. Packed out in our rucks were string, paper, pens, and other tools for making a terrain model in the middle of the woods.

Patrol gear varied from different sets of binoculars, one change of clothes and boots, night vision goggles (NVGs), smoke grenades, dud claymores, ammunition, and all the food we had packed for the week out in the field. Nothing got left behind. The rucks weighed about the same if not more than the sandbags we had run with every week. We prepped our gear for the night and set ourselves up to prepare for the worst.

We usually walked straight from the harbor site to the mission but our cadre had also coordinated with an adjacent unit for a Huey (small helicopter) to pick us up and drop us off at an insertion point. As we knelt in the snow, waiting for the Huey to arrive, the instructor grading the patrol warned us about the downwash from the propeller blades. As the Huey touched down, my whole team got knocked over with the combined weight of the rucks and the force of air from the downwash.

During Patrol Week, we were not allowed to sleep or we failed the mission. We remained awake in a state of exhaustion for the entire six days. The cadre knew that we were going to fall asleep. If they caught us sleeping, they set off their prized weapon: CS gas or riot gas.

This gas was used in the gas chamber at Boot Camp but 120 times more potent in a gas grenade. Secondly, my gas mask didn't work. Early on in Patrol Week, I stood in a cloud of CS gas after donning my gas mask and apprehensively took a deep breath to test it. My lungs erupted in pain and I uncontrollably coughed till I was blue in the face.

On the third mission, our instructor halted the patrol just before we returned to friendly lines. It was about three in the morning and he said all the teams were going to sleep for a short period of time. At the end of the rest period, he would wake us up to continue the patrol.

We had no illusion how we would be woken up. Circling up with our backs to each other, we slipped our gas masks over our heads and passed out in a matter of seconds. Every few minutes we would wake up short of breath and have to take the gas mask off to breathe but it wouldn't take long to fall back to sleep.

Sure enough, after three hours the sound of a gas grenade emitting its lethal poison pervaded our senses. "GAS! GAS! GAS!" we yelled, grabbing our gear and running for the nearest cover. After we had assembled as a group and repelled the counter-attack, we pushed on to the end of the patrol.

The exhaustion hit me in waves as I passed the first initial fatigue. I would get a second burst of energy for a few hours only to crash again. Inevitably, I fell asleep while walking, ended up talking to imaginary people, and hallucinating.

I remember one Marine trying to order pizza from a bush and swiping an imaginary card. In the middle of the week on patrol I saw a pharaoh being embalmed. Flies buzzed around Anubis as he watched over a man wrapping a dead body. It was so fantastic that I thought, "That isn't real" and wrote it off as a hallucination.

During one patrol, we circled up to let the TL and Pointman get their bearing. I saw a Marine walk out in front of me and take a knee. "Hey! Pssst! I've got this area covered," I whispered to the Marine's back. "Go find your own area!"

The Marine failed to notice and I looked to my left and right and saw Barker and Lacourse. Both the Marines on either side of me were in the right place so I looked back at the Marine in front of me – except he wasn't there.

During another patrol, the Marine in front of me stopped abruptly. Halting during a patrol is common so that the Pointman can get through some vegetation or get his bearings so I thought nothing of it. After a few minutes however, we were taught to take a knee and find cover. I walked up to the Marine still standing in the open and asked him what was going on. He woke up and suddenly realized he had fallen asleep in mid-step.

During Patrol Week, we were also given a lesson by Major Jim Land, the Marine who had recruited Carlos Hathcock for the first USMC Scout Snipers. Hathcock went on to become one of the greatest snipers the military every saw. Major Land gave us instruction on camouflage while we struggled to stay awake and give him the proper respect he deserved.

We circled up one night to hold security and my team had a rule that everyone would remain on one knee. Kneeling was more uncomfortable than sitting against a ruck and the position kept us awake. However, one night the instructor took a knee in front of me and said, "Vandekar, you are going to fall asleep. I am going to kneel right in front of you and the second you fall asleep, I'm going to gas your whole team." I tried vainly to keep my eyes open and didn't know I had nodded off until I suddenly found myself waking up to the instructor smiling at me.

If the instructor felt the team made a mistake, left gear behind, fell asleep, or committed any other infraction, he set off a CS grenade and lobbed it into the middle of the team. Immediate pandemonium ensued as we struggled to don our gas mask, grab all our gear, and flee the area.

In any case, when we heard the PFFFFFFF of the grenade, it signaled enemy contact and meant the team was compromised. Using our blanks and smoke grenades, we were directed to counter the attack, pick up wounded teammates with their gear, and evade to a secure location or rendezvous point.

Another signal for enemy contact was an artillery simulator (arty sim). These grenades whistled for a second or two then ended with a loud bang. When we heard the arty sim, we all yelled, "INCOMING!" and hit the ground.

Patrol Week was hard enough without the temperatures dropping well below freezing and even though it rained during the day, it all froze and snowed at night.

My team was on a mission involving observing a POW camp on the fourth day. While D'Errico and Lacourse went out to scout the camp, Barker and another Marine we called the Viking Warrior started to get really cold. After asking them what day of the week it was and other simple questions, I decided to huddle everyone up and call the instructor on the radio to notify him of an emergency. I couldn't tell if the two Marines were just muddled because of the sleep deprivation or if they were contracting hypothermia.

Whatever the case, the instructor agreed and we went up to the camp to huddle around the fire. Four Marines from other teams contracted hypothermia and had to be taken off the missions.

Back at the team site, Barker, an avid snowboarder and familiar with freezing temperatures, was the first to change into his dry clothes and after urging us to do the same, we all stripped down and changed. It seemed counterintuitive to remove our clothes when we were so cold, but it was extremely warm in the dry camis.

During the bridge patrol, our team was tasked with gathering information on a bridge including the depth of the water and the bottom composition. When the team asked for volunteers to go in the water, I spoke up. I constantly felt the need to prove myself to others.

We rehearsed our cold water plan before we went on patrol. We would lay our cold weather sleeping bag on the bank with a new set of dry warm clothes. I would strip down to my PT shorts and tie paracord around my waist in case I fell down so the others could pull me out. After I got out of the water, I would jump into the sleeping bag with the Viking Warrior and then put on the dry clothes.

We patrolled right up to the icy bank of the water. Looking in, I suddenly realized how serious this could become. Ice crusted the top of the water. I stripped down to my skin and we laid the sleeping bag and clothes out on the bank.

Just before I got in the water, the instructor called it off and let us know we had passed this phase. He just wanted to make sure we had a plan and were ready to execute it. As I gathered my gear and packed the sleeping bag back in the ruck, thanking my lucky stars I wouldn't have to get into the water, the instructor popped a CS grenade just for the hell of it – maybe my stars weren't that lucky.

Patrol Week culminated in an arduous 13-mile run called Escape and Evasion or E&E. Before the run we looked over ten objects for one minute, memorizing them in something known as a Kim's game. We'd played this several times during the school and knew that at some point we would have to recall the objects' appearance, shape, color, and condition.

The cadre then corralled us into a formation with our gear staged to one side. They made us sing the Marine Corps Hymn and began to pop regular, harmless smoke grenades the same color as CS gas. Nervously we held our ground, and continued drawing breath to sing. When the smoke got thick and we were unable to see, cadre began to pop CS grenades amongst the smoke grenades. As we continued singing, people begin to feel the subtle beginnings of CS poisoning and soon we were all coughing, gagging, and clawing at our eyes: E&E had begun.

Gas masks on our face, rucks squarely on our backs, and formed up as a team, we set off at a pace we hoped to endure for the entire run. The race was an individual team effort and the winning team would get a week off in Key West during the amphibious stage of training. We had no idea what to expect or how long the run would be but this confusion was all part of the test.

After the first mile, we were allowed to take our masks off and breathe freely again. We had been running with weight every Friday as part of ruck runs, so getting a pace together in the team was easy. We were familiar with this task. However, running wouldn't be the only obstacle to overcome.

Every couple of miles there was a task to complete which served as a bottleneck for the teams. Some of the tasks were radio procedures for an airstrike after assembling a radio, carrying two 5-gallon water jugs for a mile, crossing a rope bridge, and carrying a wounded Marine in a pole-less litter. The tasks were aimed at slowing us down and tiring us out. Running for hours is monotonous enough once we set our mind to it. These tasks forced us to continue to think, exercised our brain matter, and messed with our rhythm.

My team was made up of very large Marines and one very small Marine: me. The Viking Warrior gave us an advantage that helped us get through the physical challenges. When we reached the pole-less litter, they put me in as the lightest Marine. Few other teams had a Marine as light as myself. During the carry, I rehearsed aloud the ten objects to keep them fresh in our minds and kept the dialogue open.

Because of our advantage, my team came to the parked hummvees first and what we thought was the end. However, we still had to recite the ten objects from the beginning of the race. The entire team was then asked to tie eight of the thirteen knots for time, all with six days of no sleep and physical exhaustion at a maximum. Any discrepancies in the objects or knots would add time to our run. We were dehydrated, fatigued, and pushed to our mental and physical limits.

Once we completed the knots and wrote down the items, the cadre continued to harass us to drink water. They congratulated us on coming to the halfway point first. I couldn't believe it; I was dead on my feet.

We circled up within a fenced in area, took a knee and drank until our stomachs were full. The cadre made us wait until all the teams arrived so they could control the team dispersion. When all the teams had made it into the fenced in area, we formed a large circle. The cadre told us to do 25 & 5 and closed the fence gate, trapping us inside. When I had hit ten pushups, they began lobbing CS grenades over the fence. I jumped up and began to feel around for my gear while keeping my eyes shut. People were screaming and running around disoriented. Blinded with no working mask, I ran as fast as I could towards the exit, only to smash right into the fence and fall onto my back, clawing at the burning in my chest. One Marine fell on a CS grenade and began convulsing.

As I clawed at my chest and struggled to breathe, a masked Marine materialized out of the smoke with a ruck on his back and rifle in his hands. It was D'Errico! He reached down and pulled me to my feet. As I stood bent over with my hands on my knees, he lifted my ruck to my back. After I situated my ruck, he handed me my rifle and led me out of the fenced area.

My team was one of the last to get organized but once we formed up and began running again, we hit our stride. In the first couple hundred meters we passed the other teams. Guendner stood up the road pointing around the bend. As we passed him, we saw the bus waiting there, but not wanting to be deceived by yet another ARS trick, we only relaxed when we were sitting in our seats with our rucks off our shoulders. My team was the first of Guendner's teams to ever come in first.

It was an exhausting ordeal. We came back to Fort Story and slept all through the next day. Our feet were blistered and our camis and clothes were filthy. Passing Patrol Week was the crux of the school. Some people who had failed their patrols would have to come back to the school and attempt to pass again. For those of us who had passed already, the hardest stage was over. Next was the amphibious phase.

Since we were a winter class, our amphibious training took place in Key West, FL. The summer classes fin in the Chesapeake Bay. The remaining few weeks involved training on zodiac boats (small rubber rafts) and finning 1 ¼ miles each day for ten days. We had to chase a rabbit instructor even on the fins. Finning is nothing more than swimming with fins on your feet.

We took off in a military plane from Virginia and landed in Key West, FL. Each morning we woke up in our hotel rooms and took the bus to the Special Forces dive school. We got suited up in wet suits and camis for our morning fin. After each fin, we trained on boats and practiced beach attacks on civilian beaches. It was so much fun to run our boats onto the shore, pile out with our rubber rifles, and have civilians snapping pictures of us.

In the evenings, we were allowed out in Key West to eat dinner or hang out. Because my team finished first on the E&E, we were given a day off at the end of the amphibious phase to hang out in town while the other teams cleaned the boats and stowed the gear we had used. As D'Errico, Lacourse, and I drove on scooters through the town, it felt like a vacation in comparison to Patrol Week and the rest of my training in the USMC.

When we returned to Fort Story for the last time, we began packing up our supplies and getting ready for graduation. We were all given a pair of black shorts and an ARS shirt to wear. At graduation, we lined up in the morning for PT as usual, but this time our families waited across the road. We proudly wore our PT shirts with the ARS logo on the front and cami bottoms. Keith Zeier, whose ankle had totally healed, stood among us.

Our families didn't follow us, but we ran through creeks, slopping mud on ourselves, rolling in the dirt, trying to get as gruesome as possible and laughing the entire time. We finished by running up the beach towards our waiting friends and family. They saw us running through the waves, a filthy mess of ecstatic Recon Marines.

Looking back on the things I achieved, if you asked me now how I passed ARS, I wouldn't be able to tell you. They ranked us in class standing of the 33 Marines who ended up passing. I was tenth. Guendner iterated that the person who graduated 33rd still graduates an 0321. If Boot Camp was mentally exhausting, ARS was the physical equivalent. I was now the top 1 percent of the Marine Corps and had earned the right to wear the black PT shorts, but more importantly, the title of Reconnaissance Marine.

The Paddle and The Pipeline

*R*ealizing *it is my choice and my choice alone to become a Reconnaissance Marine, I accept all challenges involved with this profession. Forever shall I strive to maintain the tremendous reputation of those who went before me.*

Exceeding beyond the limitations set down by others shall be my goal. Sacrificing personal comforts and dedicating myself to the completion of the reconnaissance mission shall be my life. Physical fitness, mental attitude, and high ethics – the title of Recon Marine is my honor.

Conquering all obstacles, both large and small, I shall never quit. To quit, to surrender, to give up is to fail. To be a Recon Marine is to surpass failure; to overcome, to adapt and to do whatever it takes to complete the mission.

On the battlefield, as in all areas of life, I shall stand tall above the competition. Through professional pride, integrity, and teamwork, I shall be the example for all other Marines to emulate.

Never shall I forget the principles I accepted to become a Recon Marine: Honor, Perseverance, Spirit and Heart. A Recon Marine can speak without saying a word and achieve what others can only imagine.

This passage is the Reconnaissance Creed, taught to every Recon Marine in RTP. It's drilled into our heads just like the eleven general orders and rifle creed in Boot Camp. The first letter from each paragraph spells R-E-C-O-N. We continue to embody these traditions and virtues throughout our lives. Recon Marines that I have kept in touch with continue to give 110 percent in their jobs and school work. They seek out law enforcement, firefighter, and EMT positions to help others and set examples in every walk of life for others to follow.

The Recon Jack is another symbol that all Recon Marines become adamantly familiar with. There are many different types of Recon Jacks, but all of them embody a few of the same symbols.

The unit logo, and most common jack, has a skull centered over two paddles crossed behind it. The paddles symbolize our amphibious nature. The skull has three bullet holes symbolizing the pain, hurt, and agony Recon Marines often face in combat or training. Sometimes there is a crack in the skull representing the ability to continue with the mission despite adverse conditions.

Sometimes, if the Marine is a sniper, one of the paddles may be switched out with a sniper rifle. Other times one of the paddles may be replaced with a combat knife. There is almost always a set of wings and a re-breather from the Dräger dive rig we use when diving. Each jack depicted in a tattoo or paddle depends on the Recon Marine. Sometimes if he has not been to jump or dive school, he will abstain from including the airborne and dive symbols from his jack. Earning the jump and dive insignias are known as becoming "dual cool."

Another common symbol on a Recon Jack is the Ace of Spades. This symbol goes back to Vietnam when Recon units would staple the Ace of Spades to trees after a successful firefight or leave the card on the bodies. The Viet Cong grew to become terrified by the card. Other units in Vietnam used the Ace of Spades as well, and it became known as the Death Card.

In the 2nd Recon Battalion logo, the skull is centered on the 2nd Marine Division spearhead and stars. The stars represent Guadalcanal in the Southern Cross constellation shape. Guadalcanal was a Marine Corps victory during World War II. The jack is usually accompanied by the Recon motto: Swift, Silent, Deadly.

All reconnaissance battalions share some of these symbols or representations. For example, 3rd Recon has "celer, silens, mortalis" along the sides of their jack. This phrase is Latin for the Recon motto.

Many Recon Marines get a jack tattooed on the inside of their bicep or some other portion of their body. It identifies you to other

Marines and few civilians know what it means. Some Marines claim they are in Recon, so the tattoo brands us with the truth. Barker has one on his chest, D'Errico has one on his bicep, and I have one on my shoulder.

Marines who are killed in combat or training have their names etched onto the monument in front of the Recon office building. When entering this building, we salute not only the flag, but also the monument to the Recon Marines who have died. It is updated with each Recon Marine who gives the ultimate sacrifice.

Also etched on this memorial are the names of the 17 Recon Marines who died in the Beirut bombing. Back at the barracks in the common room sit 17 paddles wrapped and embossed with the names of the Recon casualties in Beirut. The bombing in Beirut was the largest loss of life that the Recon Community has every sustained at one time.

The tradition of paddles in the Recon Community goes way back to the early days when Recon Marines were called the Marine Raiders. The Marine Raiders were disbanded long ago, but were the original Marine Corps special operations group during World War II. They were the commandos when the USMC needed them.

This is the tradition of the paddle, as it was taught to me:

Back when Recon Marines would paddle ashore in light rafts, they would be issued a paddle as well as a rifle. The paddle was as important as the rifle, as it symbolized extract and home. Recon Marines kept it as close as their rifles.

When a Recon Marine was about to leave the unit or if he had died, his team members would clean up his paddle, sand it down, paint it, and wrap it in 550 cord. Lastly, they would present it back to him or his family and recount all the good times.

This tradition still takes place today. If a Recon Marine transfers to another unit or finishes his enlistment, his team will make him a paddle if they think he deserves one. We still sand them down, stain them, and wrap them in different 550 cord wraps. Paddles vary as much as Recon Jacks, but they usually have a plaque on the front with the dates of enlistment and some parting words. The team can put his ribbons, jump and dive insignias on it, and wood burn it with the Recon Creed if they choose. It is all artistically designed. I consider my paddle to be one of my most precious possessions.

When the team presents the paddle, it is covered or shielded from view. People gather to tell embarrassing stories about the departing Marine. At the end of the stories, the Marine responsible for making the paddle presents it to the Marine leaving. The Recon Marine leaving then shares stories about each one of the men he served with.

Part of the hype with Recon Marines is the special schools and training we get to attend. Recon Marines shoot every gun or rocket the Marine Corps has to offer, blow up all kinds of explosives, and ride in all sorts of vehicles from Hueys to zodiacs. Because of our individuality in a military dedicated to uniformity, this appearance can give other units the impression of disrespect towards the USMC and brand us as unruly cowboys with no discipline.

Camp Lejeune is a large base with over 140,000 acres of area. The main part of the base is located closest to Jacksonville with all the shops, theatre, pool, and unit barracks clustered together. But if you drove thirty minutes to the back gate you'd find the Recon community tucked away amongst some old landing zones (LZs) next to the engineers' school in Courthouse Bay. This displacement means no one has to see us and we don't have to see anyone else and that's just the way everyone likes it.

Other units with larger numbers of Marines are required to set standards to ensure that the Marines are safe and compliant with regulations. Recon units typically have more relaxed regulations involving haircuts, uniforms, and formations because there are fewer Marines to manage.

For example, on the rifle range one year, other units stood in formation in the hot sun, waiting for their leaders to tell them when to go where and the time to show up the next day. The seven other Recon Marines and I lounged in the grass in the shade with our covers off our heads. Once we were done firing, we turned in our rifles and left. We used phones to disseminate information and there were so few of us, a formation would look ridiculous. The other units didn't enjoy the fact that we didn't have to suffer like they did, and demanded we either form our own formation or join theirs.

Recon Marines go through an extensive training regimen with special insert schools, demolitions, sniper, and SERE (Survival, Escape, Resistance, and Evasion), amongst others. Not all Recon Marines get to go to each one, depending on ability, timing, and enlistment length. Sniper school is three months long, SERE is a few weeks, Dive is a few months, and attending these back to back would leave no time to go overseas and utilize the skill sets we acquired.

I managed to make it to jump school, dive school, fast rope master course, and coach's course. There were a few other miscellaneous

A CH-53 static line jump over Camp Lejeune

Bailey and I with the Dräger Lar-V oxygen rebreather

training courses such as Dragoneye unmanned aerial vehicle (UAV) and biometrics training, but these courses were just supplemental. After Marines return from a deployment, they get a period of leave followed by a training period. For Recon Marines, this training includes any schools they haven't achieved in what we call the Pipeline. After the Pipeline, we begin training for our next deployment and the cycle continues.

Once we had graduated from ARS in April 2005, we found ourselves attached to a battalion already in Iraq. There was only a skeleton crew left back in the States and we were put in a holding company to wait for everyone else to return. In the meantime, I went to Airborne school run by the Army in Fort Benning, GA in July.

Airborne school was extremely frustrating for me. We had gotten used to the small numbers and the precision in Recon training. At ARS, the cadre helped us on an individual level with a ratio of one instructor for every six to eight students. At Airborne school, we waited in formations for hours while we assembled our gear or received instruction on the next lesson. It took so long to pass along simple information like when to show up for the next day. Furthermore, the school split up the Recon Marines amongst the soldiers so there would be one Marine for each jump stick of soldiers.

Airborne is a three week course designed to teach the Army how to jump with simple parachutes out of a C-130 airplane. Army cadets and soldiers just out of Basic Training are pushed through a mass trainer to get soldiers in the sky. I felt extremely cocky straight out of ARS and with only eight or nine Marines in the mass of 400+ soldiers and cadets, my feeling of being elite magnified.

Cadets are ROTC college kids on a summer break with no military experience. With such junior Army members in the school, the cadre stopped punishments at ten pushups or ten flutter kicks. If we made a mistake, we wouldn't be doing thousands of eight-counts but told to do ten pushups.

Zeier had come with me to Airborne school and we got to know each other better. Almost every Marine at the school was Recon and it was Zeier's idea to band together and do the punishments simultaneously. During training, if someone made a mistake, the instructors would turn to the individual and tell him or her to do ten pushups. If it was one of the Marines, the Marine would turn and yell to the rest of the students "CORPSMAN UP!"

In the Marine Corps the medics, called corpsmen, are supplied by the Navy. Whenever a Marine heard the cry of "Corpsman up,"

The blade of my paddle

we'd look over and duplicate the punishment. It unified us and kept us together even though they had split us up amongst the soldiers.

The Army cadre warned us about the hills involved in their runs, but after Lochness we barely noticed we were running uphill at all. After ARS, Airborne school seemed a breeze to get through. During runs, students would fall out and drop to the back. I grabbed one particular Army student and began to pull him onward when the instructors yelled at me to let him fail the run. It was the first time in the military that someone had encouraged individualism.

In the USMC, our initial jump wings are silver with the wing tips turned inward in the fashion of the Army. The wings are called lead sleds and symbolize a five-jump chump or junior jumper. To achieve the gold wings with wings unfurled, one has to jump five more times from a second platform (helicopter), one time being at night, and two times with ruck and rifle. Because the battalion was away at war, there wasn't any competition for jump seats on the helos. I was lucky enough to pull off the gold wing requirements fairly early.

After Airborne school (August 2005), I had been in the USMC for a year and three months. I had been promised in Boot Camp that I would go to Iraq but I still saw no deployment schedule ahead of me. Due to the lack of range coaches in my battalion, I was sent to coach's course instead.

Every unit that goes to the rifle range to qualify has to provide its own coaches to teach their shooters. Recon Marines shoot regularly so the job was mostly a filler position but I enjoyed shooting and had not yet fired the Marine Corps' pistol, the M9 berretta. The coach's course was run by the Marine Corps in general, so I was away from Recon again and thrust amongst other units.

After I finished coach's course, the Battalion returned from Iraq. I went from feeling accomplished, to the new guy on campus again. All these returning Marines were heroes and war veterans while I was still trying to prove myself. They didn't care if I had jump wings or shot expert on the range. They had seen the shit and come back to talk about it. They had dust on the camis and sand in their gear. The veterans were friendly and told us some of the stories about what to expect, but they seemed untouchable.

After Iraq, the companies were split up and new companies were formed. New guys coming on board replaced the short-timers leaving to check out of the USMC. I found myself in B Company, 2nd Platoon, ironically in a team led by my team instructor at

ARS, Sergeant Guendner. He had returned to Recon Battalion and chosen me for his RTO. Also in my team were Lacourse, Jesse Freudenhammer, and Lynn Westover.

Joe Lacourse had been in RTP and ARS with me. We knew each other well and despite our first encounter, had grown to become friends. Lacourse was designated the team Pointman. Jesse Freudenhammer (Hammer) was a jacked Marine from the infantry machine gunners. He logically became our team machine gunner and had passed the ARS class after mine. Westover was a short skinny Marine with a bitter attitude. Because of his ability to carry a lot of weight despite his size, his nickname was Sherpa. He had tattoos all over his body and intimidated a lot of Marines because of his proficiency in Recon. He had been to Iraq and Afghanistan seven times. He served as our ATL and team sniper with Lacourse as his spotter.

Our team was a golden team. Our TL spent years teaching Recon; our machine gunner had served in the infantry as a machine gunner; our Pointman was a proficient navigator and driver; the ATL had experience and an extreme attention to detail that was necessary in a good sniper and ATL; and I excelled at radios.

After I had joined a team, I was sent to Fast Rope HRST Master course. I had learned to SPIE rig, rappel, and fast rope out of helicopters at ARS, so I was not too worried about finishing. HRST only lasted a few days where we tied knots and slid down a rope suspended from a helo.

Shortly after finishing HRST, the teams began training in earnest for Iraq. We trained on Camp Lejeune and shot on many ranges to become proficient in weapons systems. We also began to learn what the country would be like both culturally and environmentally.

It was January 2006 when we went to 29 Palms, CA to train in the desert and test what we had learned. There is a mock town set up at 29 Palms complete with a bank, mosques, residential district, graveyard, market, and anything else you can imagine. The USMC had about 50 Iraqi nationals along with over 300 Marines acting as Iraqis at 29 Palms to make it as realistic as possible.

This training exercise lasted several weeks and taught us in-depth improvised explosive device (IED) recognition and room clearing. We fine tuned our platoon and team skills. At the end of the training, we conducted several days' worth of live operations with our entire unit from the lowest PFC to the highest colonel working to prevent insurgents in the mock town from succeeding in their mission.

When we flew back to Camp Lejeune, everyone had a clear picture of what to expect, but those of us who hadn't been to Iraq weren't sure exactly what it would be like. We were given thirty days of leave to go home and say goodbye to our family and loved ones.

When we returned from leave, we were mentally and physically ready to deploy. I had trained for almost two years straight for this very moment. I could taste it. I had been fine-tuned by the USMC to go overseas and survive alone and unafraid in a Recon team. I expected the worst but at the end of the day, I had no idea what I was in for.

Iraq – Round One

I must admit that looking back on Iraq, it seems that on an individual level, the country kicked my ass. As a junior Marine heading into Iraq, I expected to kill my enemy in a massive three hour shootout, just like Hollywood showed. However, the enemy attempted to remain discreet when attacking and, if caught in the open, denied everything and rarely fought back.

After getting off the plane at Al Taqaddum (or TQ for short), I looked around me at the landscape, but being on a military base, there wasn't much "Iraq" to actually see. We waited for a few days for our ride to Camp Fallujah. We would be stationed at Camp Fallujah for the seven month deployment.

All convoys from TQ to Camp Fallujah were driven through the city of Fallujah. The city was controlled by the U.S., but many firefights and mortars took place there. For this reason, convoys were conducted at night when the Marine Corps had the advantage.

The team leaders, platoon sergeants, and other leadership roles had already convoyed to Camp Fallujah. Alpha Co. was flying in shortly behind us on a plane so we waited for the trucks to return. On the evening of the convoy, we stood on base next to the road in formation, hanging out with our rucks for the 7-tons to arrive. It felt like PT at ARS all over again.

We had been briefed on which trucks we would be loading, so when the 7-tons pulled up, we headed to the trucks and reported to whoever was accountable for us. We sat in the back, chatting about what to expect. A few minutes later, when everyone had been accounted for, the convoy lurched, roared, and turned around for the drive to Camp Fallujah.

We had been given one magazine and crammed in the back of a 7-ton truck which resembles an 18-wheeler. The armor of a 7-ton comes just over my forehead so none of us could comfortably look over the lip. We hadn't been issued our night vision yet so we couldn't see anything anyway. Nevertheless, just like the bus ride to Boot Camp, my nerves were taut and I was anxious for the unexpected.

At some point during the convoy, the trucks came to a halt. While the trucks waited and idled, I remember peeking over the lip of the armor tentatively, catching my first glimpse at the landscape of Iraq. She was like a celebrity to me. I saw nothing but a few lights on a nearby building, but in my anticipation of a completely foreign culture, I wildly speculated on the purpose behind the buildings. "Was that one a market place? Is that where people live?" I scanned for insurgents. Shadows appeared sinister and as dogs barked, my senses elevated.

The trip to Camp Fallujah concluded unceremoniously. As we pulled into the camp, I jumped down off the trucks, grabbed my gear, and followed my team members to the cans.

The cans were little rooms where Marines slept. Most of the units slept in one location with rows and rows of trailers pushed end to end protected by high concrete barriers. Bunkers reinforced with sandbags stood at the end of every other row. Sandbags lined the walls of the rooms and loose stone carpeted the ground to prevent against mud building up during rain. I slept with Hammer and Lacourse in a room probably 12'x10'. Across from us in the next set of trailers were Sherpa and Guendner.

We were lucky; our room had been furnished with a TV and DVD player that the previous Recon battalion (Bn) had left behind. During the deployment, when we were back on base, Chris Berg (our corpsman) and Lacourse crowded into our room to watch DVDs. A big favorite was the TV series called Desperate Housewives. Don't judge, it was the only DVD we had.

During my very first night in Iraq, after we had picked our rooms and settled down to catch some sleep, artillery began firing from base. The artillery battery was located near our cans so all the walls shook and the explosions vibrated our eardrums.

"Oh SHIT! Hammer, is that incoming?!" I yelled down to

Hammer from my top bunk. He had been here before, so I expected him to know.

"I have no idea!" he yelled back.

"Should we be in that bunker at the end of our row of cans?" Lacourse asked.

"Guendner will come and get us if we should be somewhere," Hammer reasoned. We lay back, uneasy through the pounding of the artillery guns. We had no idea what was going on. It was a rough welcoming.

We never got used to it. After I had been through a couple months, I was walking back from the showers as Smykowski, a Recon Marine from another platoon, was walking towards them. Unannounced, the artillery started firing again and we both ducked instinctively and glanced at the other. Realizing we had shared this natural fear, we started laughing.

We didn't get to Iraq with balls of steel. Hammer warned me, "The first dead body you see will shock you. The first dead Marine you see will scare you. The first dead friend you see will fuck you up." When we responded to an incident as a quick reaction force (QRF), we saw our friends lying on the ground in splints and bandages. It was tough seeing these Marines down on the ground with a ticket home. Everyone seemed crucial and critical to the mission. We couldn't spare anyone.

Our missions kept us out in the field for several days at a time. We varied the tactics based on what was asked of us. Generally though, Recon was asked to conduct a specific type of mission.

Reconnaissance Battalions have two distinct specialties; raids to kill or capture High Value Individuals (HVIs) and Observation Posts (O.P.s) to gather information to generate intelligence.

A raid occurred when we knew the location of an HVI and HQ decided they wanted to take him out of the equation. We went to the location, killed the insurgents there or took them with us for further questioning. The key to a successful raid was speed, surprise, and violence of action. Simply put, this tactic meant we wanted to be quick, catch the enemy with his guard down, and keep the enemy off-guard with continuous aggressive action.

An O.P. is the precursor to a raid. In order to know the location of an HVI, we first watched the house, confirmed he lived there, and frequented the establishment. We took back information such as pictures, notes, vehicle descriptions, etc. to the intelligence shop known as the S-2. The S-2 then consolidated this information with other information from other sources and generated a comprehensive intelligence picture that was used in briefings and updates. Sometimes the intelligence was sent directly back to the team on the O.P. and they moved straight into a raid.

In a simpler case, another unit may discover the location of an HVI and pass on the intelligence to the USMC. Some units specialized in signals, others specialized in demolitions. My unit specialized in raids. If the USMC found an HVI, they usually gave it to Recon to handle.

However, having two specialties didn't limit us to two tasks. As Sherpa pointed out regularly, we were a "jack of all trades, master of none." We could be utilized to hold security, conduct IED sweeps, find weapon caches, and anything else a unit commander needed help doing. We had fewer boots on the ground than an infantry unit, but we were better trained and better equipped.

During my first deployment, 2nd Recon Bn was put in charge of the area south of Fallujah called the Zaidon. This area had not had any coalition forces in it for several years so it was either a safe haven for terrorists or neglected by both sides. When the USMC wants to find out, they send in a reconnaissance unit.

When we first moved into an area, it usually went one of two ways. It could be quiet for weeks or months before a commander determined from our intel that there were no insurgents. The area had no coalition forces but no insurgents had moved in either: NTR, nothing to report. Or the insurgents could be using the area for their stockpile of weapons to use on U.S. troops in other areas. We could move into the area and upset their cozy hideout, while the terrorists had to get as much contraband out as they could before we seized it. This latter example was the case for the Zaidon.

Being in charge of the Zaidon meant we not only conducted raids and O.P.s but also talked to the locals, established rapport with the village elders, and kept the conversation open between higher-ups and the Iraqis in need. A lot of the old school Recon Marines complained about this work, seeing these tasks as a grunt unit's job with more resources and man power to spread out. But our Battalion Commander's philosophy was "we wash windows," meaning we would do everything from the mundane to the exciting. What he hoped was a favorable perspective from other units towards Recon. If they wanted something done more along the special operations line, they wouldn't hold a grudge against us or our attitude.

Because of our willingness to stand ground and hold territory in Iraq like an infantry unit, 2nd Reconnaissance Bn was asked by other units to conduct raids. Early on in the deployment we received intelligence of a terrorist cell within a cluster of six buildings. A unit had received this information but was not comfortable with hard entries and raid tactics. That's where we came in.

It was the first raid of the deployment. The Battalion Commander gave it to B Co. and B Co. gave it to my platoon. The platoon filed into the briefing room at around 0900 to hear about our next mission.

"There is a known insurgent stronghold at this location," began the Platoon Commander. Seated at the center of the room were the TLs and around the edges were the members of each team. At the front stood the Lieutenant, briefing from PowerPoint slides.

"Our platoon has been tasked with raiding these six houses. The enemy most likely course of action is to stand and fight. We'll be driving in using our own hummvees. Guendner, your team will be the first team to hit the houses. After that, we'll improvise and adapt with whoever is available. Guendner, who in your team will be first on the door?"

Guendner looked around. Lacourse was our driver, so he would remain with the vehicle. Hammer would be situated in the turret and providing overwatch with his machine gun. That left Sherpa, the ATL, Guendner, the TL, and me.

"Vandekar," Guendner replied.

My Platoon Commander looked towards me and nodded. "Vandekar, are you alright with that?" he asked.

"Yes, sir," I replied. I was one of the most junior Marines in the platoon. I was asked to be the first on the door in the first house on the first raid on my first deployment. What was I supposed to say? Initially I wasn't afraid, but I got there.

When I returned from Iraq, people asked me all the time about fear, whether or not I was afraid, and whether or not fear was a good thing. Like nervousness, fear can be both a good and bad thing. One can be scared enough to run away or one can be scared enough to be courageous. After all, one can't be courageous if one is never afraid of anything. It might seem courageous to run into a house where people had guns and were trying to kill us, but if we weren't afraid, courage didn't play a factor.

We briefed in the afternoon on communication procedures, adjacent units, the enemy most likely course of action, and which team would hit which house in a perfect scenario. Not one raid that I've ever been on went as planned. It is impossible to foresee every factor in a raid. Despite the unpredictability of a raid, it is important to plan out what will happen on the ground so everyone has a rough sketch of what is expected. Even though we would plan on a certain person kicking in a certain door, being adaptable to the situation is crucial to the raid success.

We prepped our gear in the evening. We made sure our magazines were clean and topped off. We ensured our NODs (Night Optical Devices) had fresh batteries, and we switched our ACOG (2x zoom scope) for an aim point or Eotech (red dot sight). We configured our gear for quick and quiet movement and made sure we had red and green chemlights to mark rooms and houses. We rehearsed magazine changes and room clearing techniques within our teams. We discussed suspect detention methods and talked through different scenarios. We prepped the slings on the sledge hammers, battering rams, and crowbars.

As the sun set, the day seemed to go just as any other day in Iraq went. We went to the chow hall and ate dinner. We watched a DVD or went to the phone center to call our families. During the mundane tasks that made up our routines, the realization of what was about to happen set in. I had already been in the field several times, but now I was going in to get someone who was willing to fight about it.

The raid location was a set of six houses adjacent to a road elevated on a berm. The first building closest to the road was to be the first one hit – my target. I was supposed to get out of the truck and hightail it to the door. I would stack on the door and after someone smashed it in with a sledge, I would make entry.

The first person to enter a room usually moves along the wall adjacent to the door to the nearest corner. He is called the rabbit. The second man in the room moves along the other adjacent wall as the people inside shoot at the rabbit. Ideally, the second man is able to shoot the defenders before they are able to get a bead on the rabbit.

Though I was briefed on the route, I remember nothing of the trip. It seemed as though we just suddenly arrived at the houses. The drivers killed the engines of the trucks and the turret gunners looked down from the elevated road into the cluster of houses. The enemy most likely course of action was to fight, but looking down into the quiet homes, it didn't seem like anyone was moving. Was this because they were asleep or simply hiding in ambush?

I had fixed my bayonet to the seat in front of me. Guendner

advised against using it, pointing out I would probably hurt myself before I did any good with it.

I hopped out of the truck and we ran down the path to the first building. I peered into the darkness with my eyes wide open. I scanned the adjacent windows and rooftops expecting a shadow to dart across an alcove. Concertina wire (a sort of barbed wire) strewn across the road channeled our movement down into the houses. It was nerve-wracking being forced to funnel through one section. Everything seemed to be watching us. Had we arrived silently?

As I stepped up to the door of the first house, the Marine with the sledge stood opposite me. I kept my concentration on the door in case it should be opened from the inside while I waited for the signal from Sherpa behind me. He gave the nod to the sledge. Two robust hits later, I was inside a small entry room with Sherpa close on my tail end. Facing us was an unarmed Iraqi male shielding his eyes against our lights. Sherpa tackled him and I stepped up, placed my knee in his back and zip-tied his wrists. Other Marines pushed past us into the house. I had expected to freeze up but my instincts had kicked in before I had time to think about what I would do.

As we pushed into the rest of the house, I found myself again with Sherpa in a second room full of sleeping Iraqi males. I counted seven. I couldn't see if they held rifles under the covers and my heart began beating faster. Should I push into the room to lift up the blankets? Should I remain quiet? Sherpa again took action.

"WAKE THE FUCK UP! LET ME SEE YOUR HANDS! SHOW ME YOUR HANDS, MOTHER FUCKER!" Sherpa yelled. He shined his white light directly into the eyes of the males, disorienting them and preventing them from seeing how many Marines were in the room. I joined in the fray, yelling commands in English, despite the fact that they probably didn't understand. Through the confusion we kept them off their guard.

There were several males in each house. We found rifles, cell phones, and other contraband, and if the concertina wire was any indication, these houses were a training camp for insurgents. We detained the men, took pictures, names, and information, and sent them back to base for questioning.

It turned out that the Zaidon was not a friendly place to be. Situated in the east of the infamous Al Anbar province just below Fallujah, it was a critical rural area close to the cities where the insurgents could stage their equipment and attacks.

During the deployment, I kept a log of the injuries and deaths of people in my unit. I left my log on base so the notepad would not slip out and compromise any names in the field. This security measure meant I had to resort to memory to write the casualties down inside the wire. Within two months I had written this entry:

"I can't write everyone who gets hurt. May 17th and there are too many."

We had lost four Marines so far due to an IED and others had been injured in gunfights and explosions. The area was so hostile that we weren't able to expose ourselves for more than a few minutes without attracting some sort of small arms fire. We began sandbagging the roof and windows against sniper and mortar fire. The mortars were so regular, that my team would take bets on the exact minute they would land.

"Twenty dollars says the first one will land at 16:38." We had a theory that when the terrorists got off their day job, they'd switch to the night-shift of lobbing rounds at the Americans. Mortar rounds always landed around happy hour.

On one particular instance, I was standing up on rooftop for my four hour watch. As the sun crept over the house, the shade spilled onto my side of the roof. Due to the intense heat, I decided to rest in the shade. The problem was that the shade lay away from the bullet proof glass we had setup.

An hour after I had stepped away from the glass, someone took a pot-shot which hit the wall behind my head. All I heard was the sharp crack of the round hitting the wall. If one is not looking in the direction of the shot the second it is fired, it can be extremely difficult to locate the shooter. If the sound echoes off of buildings, the only indication of direction is the flash of the muzzle.

The Battalion sent out one company at a time, rotating A Co. out while B Co. remained in the wire (on base) and vice versa. We overlapped a few days at a time so there would be no gaps in the coverage.

Generally, we drove out in the middle of the night to a predetermined house. We knew the area we wanted to work and we picked a house using satellite imagery. The house was set back from the road and maintained a standoff distance from the others around it. Most importantly, it was central to the area we wanted to learn about. Other factors included being able to communicate with higher headquarters and easy access to a main road.

When we rolled up to a house, one team jumped straight up to rooftop security with sniper rifles, machine guns, bullet proof glass, sandbags, binoculars, and other essential gear. One dismounted team helped Lieutenant with the locals, while a third team remained in the turrets of the vehicles until the rooftop was setup. Lastly, the final team picked a room to sleep in and passed out as quickly as possible. This team was the first to patrol the neighborhood as soon as Lieutenant wanted to familiarize the locals with our presence and look for anything immediately out of the ordinary. Sometimes that patrol was immediate. Other times it began at first light.

We rolled up to the house already knowing which team would be doing what. We gave the owners five to ten minutes to take what they needed and go to their neighbors.

The villages we worked in were all interrelated so the neighbors were very close relatives. We also cleaned up the place and left a nice chunk of change and any leftover food and water we had brought with us. While it was inconvenient to displace them from the home, we weren't barbarians storming in to ransack the pantry and break all the windows. There was a level of civility to the whole procedure.

When we left the wire to find a house, our hummvees were stuffed full of water in every crevice that wasn't occupied by ammunition and gear. We held the house (called a firm base) for as long as our supplies lasted. Usually we ran out of water first because it was so hot.

We were able to remain in the field without a resupply for about seven to ten days while we conducted all our missions from the firm base in the surrounding area. The terrorists knew we were there and we knew they were around, but it was our dismounted patrols that were the key to the whole equation.

The dismounted patrols left a light footprint and were difficult to track. A dismounted team had the capability to remain alone for up to 72 hours and packed enough firepower to take on a much larger force. They could send pictures via satellite or HF communications. When covert, these patrols located mortar teams, tracked smuggled weapons, found HVIs, and most importantly, countered the constant IED threat in the area.

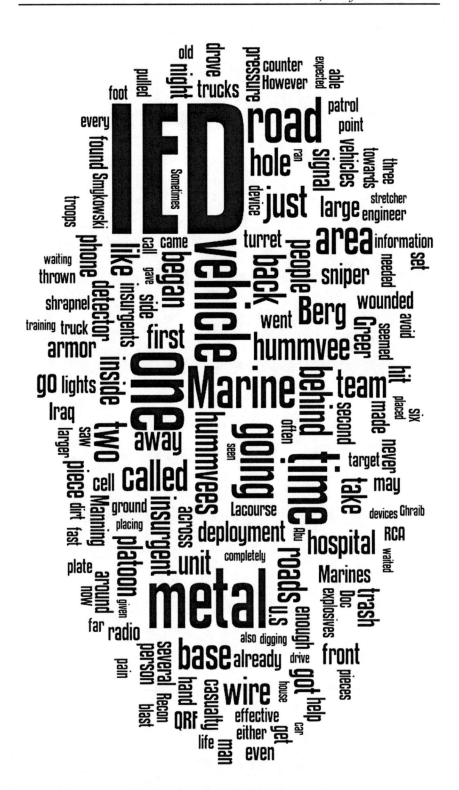

IEDs

I had trained for a few weeks at 29 Palms, California in preparation for the conditions in Iraq. The desert in California wasn't exactly like the desert overseas, and the seasons had been completely opposite. Trust the USMC to send me to train in the winter in order to get me ready for a summer deployment and vice versa.

At 29 Palms, we learned about IEDs; tricky homemade explosives that could be made from a soda can, MRE sleeve, or even a dead carcass. I thought I would be walking into Iraq tiptoeing around every piece of debris. I knew what to look for, but because of the diverse nature of IEDs, it seemed they could be hidden in any piece of trash and in Iraq, trash was plentiful.

IEDs come in three basic configurations. They can be detonated directly by wire to an electrical switch. This type of detonation requires an insurgent to be on the scene and endangers his life to U.S. troops. On the other hand, because the electrical signal has a direct hard-line to the explosives, it is nearly impossible to counter the signal without actually cutting the wire.

The second type is very similar, but the switch is replaced by a communications device: either a walkie-talkie or cell phone. The cell phone receives a signal and sends the current to the explosive. This way, the insurgent can call the device from farther away and be safe from incrimination. Unfortunately for him, the U.S. troops have effective counter-jamming methods and are able to prevent the device from receiving the mortal transmission. On the other hand, if the insurgent is able to set it off, he can't be considered guilty for simply holding a cell phone in his hand.

The third kind of IED is the hardest to detect, the hardest to counter, and the hardest to pin on anyone: the pressure plate. Two metal plates, sometimes as small as a garden hose, carry opposite charges. When coalition forces drive over the two pieces, the metal connects and sends a charge to the explosive. No one is around to set it off, and because of the direct connection, jamming doesn't work. Fortunately, these devices have to be buried close to the surface to avoid the weight of the soil setting these suckers off prematurely. Insurgents lay the two plates down, cover them with a loose line of sand, and leave what we call a "snail trail," due to the appearance of the raised sand.

The most common countermeasure to the pressure plates is just to let them go off. To do this, we employ rollers. Rollers sit a few yards in front of a vehicle and consist of many wheels. The rollers are heavy enough to set the charge off and far enough in front to keep everyone inside the vehicle safe.

IEDs are mostly emplaced to target vehicles such as hummvees and tanks due to the larger number of people inside of the vehicle. Unfortunately, the IEDs are just as effective against people on foot. The quantity of explosives inside the IED designates the intended target of the IED. A larger IED will be emplaced to target a vehicle, because a smaller IED made out of a mortar round would be ineffective.

During my first deployment, we had an engineer named Greer attached to us on missions. Having an engineer allowed us to clear our own route into an area of operations and not wait for coordination with a separate engineer unit. We swept every single dirt road with metal detectors. Paved roads, or hardball, are not as much of a threat and we just had to look out for old blast craters from IEDs called scabs.

Scabs usually had left over metal in the crater which would cause the metal detector to go off. They were a pain to clean and insurgents enjoyed placing IEDs in the scabs because of the amount of time it took to find them. Only a patient Marine will stop, take his time, and clean it out, all the time unaware that someone may be watching with a cell phone. It was often easier to just avoid the craters altogether.

We had an extra metal detector so I helped Greer sweep the road; two is one, one is none. There were copious amounts of metal on dirt roads ranging from pieces of rebar near bridges to old soda cans and even old IED shrapnel. So when I got a beep signal on the metal detector I assessed the size and strength of the signal and decided if it was a threat.

First, I kicked around with my feet to uncover any gum wrappers, aluminum cans or pieces of metal that may have set off the detector on the surface. If I still got a fairly large beep from the speaker of the metal detector, I began digging – carefully. At some point I was going to uncover a piece of metal pipe, a weapons cache, or an IED. But to avoid digging a six foot hole, I continually swept the metal detector over the hole I was digging to direct my efforts. Most of the time it ended up being trash but I wasn't going to wave six hummvees forward on a hunch.

Greer and I were sweeping down a dirt road when we found an old IED crater. Typically, we'd take turns jumping in and sweeping for IEDs. We couldn't navigate the trucks around this one because it was the only dirt road into the area and all the trucks were behind us.

During this particular instance, it was my turn to jump down. I began clearing out the hole as Greer continued sweeping ahead, occasionally glancing backward to see how I was doing. He doubled back at one point to give me a hand as I was finding lots of little pieces of jagged metal. It all had to be removed because each piece collectively gave off a large beep. This hole was beginning to be a pain in the ass.

Greer pointed out the little box in the corner by my foot first. He stepped down softly and I got out and let the expert do his job. After carefully lifting it up and moving some rocks, he saw that it was connected to a mortar round and we called in an entire engineer crew. Our hummvees were a hundred yards behind us on security and they surrounded the area to prevent traffic from approaching. "From now on," Greer said, holding the mortar round now cut away from the pressure plate wires. "I'm jumping into every hole."

When we found an IED, the first step was to move away and secure the area. We didn't want any Iraqis to get hurt either. We never knew if the IED was about to go off or if there were other IEDs strung up beside it. After we secured the area, we called the engineers who specialize in blowing things up. They either removed the IED to take back to base as intelligence or detonated it in place.

In the case of this pressure plate, it wouldn't have mattered if an insurgent was watching or not, as he was completely dependent on me stepping on his trap.

Sometimes they emplaced the IEDs in three steps. The first person dug a hole and left. The second person placed the IED in the hole with wires trailing out. The last person brought the trigger device and rigged the whole thing to go off. Sometimes the IED had an RCA adaptor on the end like the kind you plug into the back of a TV. The third person walked up with a wire and a simple RCA jack and plugged it in. Maybe only one of these men (or kids) was an insurgent. The insurgents inevitably coerced the others through threats or money to carry out this task.

Sean Manning, an ATL with one of the teams, was on a dismounted patrol midway through the deployment. He and his team were avoiding roads due to the IED threat when he came across a piece of wire trailing along the ground. One end of the wire trailed towards the road where three roads intersected into a T junction. Manning scanned along the wire which lay amongst some tall reeds and trash looking for the connector or IED.

As he followed the wire, he came across a phone base station with the RCA adapter connected to it. Wires continued through the trash towards the T in the road where Donoho, a 6′ 8″ machine gunner from a separate team, was walking across the intersection.

As a sniper and senior member of the platoon with multiple combat deployments, Manning was an extremely capable Recon Marine. Relying on his instincts and the knowledge he had received from previous devices, Manning decided to disconnect the RCA connector and wires.

Within moments of disconnecting the base, it lit up with bright colorful lights and started blaring a tune. It startled Manning so much he dropped the unit, scrambled up the incline through the trash to the road, and raised his arms, turning in circles, showing whoever was watching him the middle finger. The momentary delay from the cell phone call connecting to the base station was the difference between Donoho living or becoming "pink mist."

Because of the increasing effectiveness of IEDs, coalition troops began armoring their hummvees. The more we armored, the larger the IEDs got. However, at some point the IEDs were going to be too big to bury covertly or the hummvees were going to be too heavy to drive effectively.

The U.S. answered the hummvee problem by adding an additional vehicle to the U.S. armament called the Mine Resistant Ambush Protection vehicle (MRAP) or the Cougar. This vehicle was specifically designed as a countermeasure against IEDs. The bottom

Greer and I sweeping for IEDs on dirt roads

An artillery round used in an IED with det-cord protruding

of the MRAP was V-shaped to deflect the blast and armor was built into the structure. hummvees were already too heavy and slow to continue strapping armor to them.

As a result of the MRAP, the enemy began making more effective explosives. A new IED, which launched a specially formed high-velocity projectile, was found in the east in 2006. It was designed to hit the drivers and passengers inside the hummvee with extremely hot, liquid metal projectiles. This IED was set off by movement or metal and was aimed at the windows of vehicles. The liquid metal went through armor like butter.

To counter this new IED, the U.S. came out with the rhino. The rhino was a large block of metal which sat on a pole several yards in front of the hummvee. It triggered the IEDs to go off early and the shrapnel harmlessly missed the trucks – simple, but effective. The insurgent groups in the east fighting the Army never shared this technology with the insurgent groups in the west fighting the Marine Corps, and I never encountered any IEDs like this one.

Another tactic which the insurgents began using was secondary IEDs. Secondary IEDs utilize the original IED to stop or slow down a vehicle or convoy. When more troops come forward to help protect and aid the wounded, a secondary IED goes off. Or an IED may be rigged to blow up with two or three others all strung in a line. We might find one IED and back off 100 meters only to find out we're sitting on a second tied to the first! We spaced our vehicles and foot patrols out so if one of us were to get hit there would be minimum casualties. It sounded like a good idea but it hid the fact that someone was still lying down 100 meters ahead, bleeding out.

The best way to counter any IED was to catch it before it even hit the ground. We gathered information by questioning locals and asking them about their surrounding area. Rarely would an IED blow up outside a guilty person's house. After all, the owner of the house was also likely to be hurt by the blast. But the owner may have seen who placed the IED there in the first place. If we got no information we'd try to watch at night at crucial intersections when we expected the insurgents were emplacing the IEDs in the ground.

During one rooftop watch, a sniper in Bailey's platoon saw a man pull up at night past curfew (10:00 pm) on the side of the road. The man got out of his car, removed something from his trunk and moved to the far side of the road. He bent down and began to use the object in some manner hidden by his body. It appeared he was placing an IED, but the sniper had a bad feeling about it. He placed a

An old IED crater or scab which concealed a second IED

Mortar rounds buried in order to make IEDs

.50 cal bullet from the Barrett sniper rifle through the engine of the car and we went to investigate.

It turned out that the objects from the car were buckets and the man was coming out at night to fill up his water at the canal on the side of the road. He was innocent, but from our perspective he had been placing an IED. Thanks to the excellent judgment from the sniper, this man lived, but would the sniper have been ethically wrong if he had taken the shot and killed him?

IEDs are a nightmare scenario for any unit. We drove around at a medium pace for fear of going too fast and not seeing one, but not so slow as to be an easy target. It was hard to gauge the appropriate speed and a lot of the time it depended on the circumstances.

My team was on QRF one night when we were called to aid in the casualty evacuation (cas-evac) of another unit. QRF acts as a 911 force for any trouble that may arise.

"QRF! QRF!" The cry came from the ROC (Radio Operations Center). Whoever had called on the radio needed backup and they had called us. My team was wide-eyed in fractions of a second. Throwing our armor over our heads and grabbing our rifles, we ran out to the hummvees staged by the front of the house. We all knew which truck we were assigned to in case of emergencies. We had already planned out where we were sitting and who would be standing behind the machine gun in the turret or driving.

Guendner ran to the ROC to get details on what was happening and where. The rest of us went over our gear, double checking our NODs, radios, and starting the trucks. We would yell out things that we had just remembered as if we were going down a large checklist as a group:

"Don't forget to keep your radios on platoon net, 674!"

"AA batteries?!"

"Here. Lacourse, you need some zip-ties for handcuffs?"

"No, I picked some up from inside."

The chatter continued, each of us going over our own shopping list of to-dos and helping each other out. We had no idea what the QRF was for: a firefight or a wounded Marine. We just had to prepare for anything. Moments later, Guendner emerged with the platoon corpsman, Doc Berg.

"Doc's coming with us. A unit was passing through our area and got hit by an IED. They have several casualties so we're going to help med-evac back to Abu Ghraib."

Recon corpsmen are very different from your average Marine

Corps corpsmen. Special Amphibious Reconnaissance Corpsmen, or SARCs, go through an extensive two year training regimen complete with emergency room time, practicing on live animals, and endless hours of academic work. Their training often takes as long as two years before they are ready to deploy.

They serve side-by-side with Recon Marines and go through ARS just like the rest of us. They patrol, raid, and stand in the turrets just like the Recon Marines but they also have the added responsibility of caring for the lives of the Marines in the platoon. Lacourse and Berg were good friends so when our team went out on patrol, Berg often accompanied us. He was one of the best SARCs I have ever seen.

We roared the two trucks out of the defenses of the firm base, replacing the barbed wire and static defenses behind us. We reached the site of the explosion in a few moments. Berg dismounted and ran out to assist where he could. I sat behind the passenger side monitoring the radio. Joe Lacourse sat at the wheel and turned the truck towards the military hospital, Abu Ghraib, while we waited.

Over the chatter of the radio, I heard the progress they were making. It seemed there were two Marines in bad condition. One was classified as urgent surgical, which meant he was expected to die in an hour if not treated surgically soon. We would take him in our convoy. Doc Berg did not have the tools to save his life but could buy him time and take away the pain. The other one was a priority casualty, expected to die in four to six hours if not treated. He would be taken to the hospital by the unit hit by the IED. Berg had already corrected several mistakes their corpsman had made and began stabilizing the Marines for movement.

Normally, we would call a med-evac chopper to fly them out of the area. However, a helicopter takes time to get up in the air. Using a helo is advantageous if we are far from a base, but we were less than thirty minutes and my unit had been nearby when they were hit. By the time a helicopter made it to the site of the IED explosion, we would already be more than halfway to the hospital. Still, this Marine did not have a lot of time and we waited tensely in the first truck for the signal from Berg.

We drove in Iraq without lights at night to mask our presence. Utilizing our NODs and infrared headlights to see the roads, we gave off no ambient light to the naked eye. However, this time we needed to drive as fast as possible so we needed our white lights on. It was a seesaw decision between getting the wounded back as quickly as we could and avoiding getting ourselves blown up by driving recklessly on IED-filled roads. Also, the faster we drove, the harder it would be for Doc to work on the casualty while riding.

"T-Cup, we're ready to push back here," Sherpa called over the radio.

"Roger, pushing," I responded. "PUNCH IT, JOE!" We drove between thirty-five and forty-five mph, swerving to avoid potholes which could disguise an IED and compound our problems.

As we approached our firm base, which we intended on passing, our company 1st Sergeant stepped out into the road to stop us. We screeched to a halt, wondering if somewhere else, somebody needed help.

"Why are you going so fast?" he asked reproachfully.

"WE'VE GOT AN URGENT CASUALTY IN OUR--," Guendner began to yell, but realizing his mistake, 1st Sergeant waved us on.

Seconds turned to minutes as Lacourse peered over the steering wheel into the dark night. I can only imagine the wounded Marine's thoughts. Was he thinking of his family? Was he blinded by the pain he was feeling? Did he think he was going to live? I hoped Doc had given him enough drugs to knock him out and prevent him from thinking at all.

We pulled into the Abu Ghraib road, tearing up the path. A guard would be waiting at the gate to take our unit's name and how many vehicles were entering. However, I had already called ahead on the radio and told the gate our situation. Because we had a casualty, he waved us through forgiving the normal procedures.

My vehicle pulled up by the hospital where four or five people waited with stretchers. Industrial-sized lights bathed the large asphalt area where there was enough room to pull in several hummvees.

I yelled to the medical personnel as I jumped out of the hummvee, beckoning them towards the second vehicle coming in quickly behind us. A stretcher was pulled up and I stood transfixed. I hadn't seen this Marine yet. He was still anonymous, but once they put him on the waiting stretcher and pulled him from behind the open door of the hummvee, he would become real.

I saw Berg frantically relaying information and treatment that he had given the casualty. He reported what drugs were now running through the critically wounded Marine and gave the waiting staff a step-by-step account of his progress so they would know where to pick up treatment. They would not have to start diagnosing at square one.

The hospital staff wheeled the limp body away from the door, and I saw a blurry, dark, disfigured shape. The tattered clothing mixed in with shredded flesh. His arm was clearly missing, but where it was torn was difficult to tell. I couldn't distinguish whether his leg was gone as well, but it didn't look like he'd be able to use it anyway. The Marine was either passed out, in shock, or too far gone to know what was going on. His clothes, the stretcher, his flesh: it was all a dark, bloody mass.

As the shadows of the people hovering over him played across his mangled body, he became real, almost a monster. He was everything I feared; to be maimed or disfigured by a faceless enemy while in Iraq. I watched, hypnotized, unable to pull away from this man I didn't know, but was so suddenly close to.

As he disappeared into the hospital, we packed into our hummvees a little slower. The gate didn't seem to rise as fast as when we had entered. We drove back into the field, taking our time on the roads now, lights off. We were sober with the realization that just an hour before, a Marine in the same position driving on these same roads had his life changed forever.

He would never teach his son to swing a bat. He would never fully embrace his mother again. He would learn to eat with one hand. He would probably be confined to a wheelchair and his family would grieve over his sacrifice. Hell, he might not even live.

During the same deployment, 1st platoon sent out two vehicles on a mounted reconnaissance mission on the outskirts of the area we worked in. After the necessary information was gathered and several locals had been talked to, the team returned to their firm base.

The six hours that the team had been on patrol had given the insurgents enough time to emplace a pressure plate IED behind them. The lead vehicle struck the IED directly underneath the front passenger where the TL, Mark Smykowski, was seated.

Smykowski was immediately thrown from the vehicle across a canal. The interpreter, directly behind the front passenger, also was propelled from the vehicle, but fell into the canal where he drowned. The driver, a Marine named Freeman, was thrown in the opposite direction and crushed most of the bones on his right side.

The turret gunner, Chris Brink, a Marine I had been in RTP and ARS with, was thrown from the turret. As he collided with the machine gun in the turret, he broke his jaw. When he landed, he broke both his legs, severed his Achilles heal, and crushed the bones in his feet.

When help arrived, Brink was found conscious and propping himself up on his elbows in order to breathe. Freeman was unconscious but alive. They were able to help him regain consciousness, though he would pass out again at the field hospital. He would later awaken on the plane to Bethesda, MD. Smykowski, the team leader, died that day.

I had not known Smykowski as a friend, only from reputation. I had trained for the deployment with him as we served in the same company. He was one of the senior veterans who seemed larger than life and untouchable. Despite the fact that he had no responsibility for my training, he had taken the time to personally show me how a Russian anti-aircraft gun worked that his platoon had brought back to base.

We sent too many people home in caskets from IEDs. Sometimes the killer was the shrapnel tearing through an up-armored hummvee. Other times it was purely the shock wave passing through and stopping someone's heart. Other people stood on a hummvee-destroying IED when the IED went off and have walked away unscathed. It was left up to God if an IED was going to kill, take a leg, or leave you alone.

During 2006, my vehicle served as the point vehicle for most of the deployment. We found over eighteen IEDs, both large and small, with a myriad of trigger devices. Driving down the road was completely different after experiencing the awesome power that these inanimate objects hold. Now every piece of rubble or hole in the ground made us cringe and cup our balls.

Despite all the armor in the hummvee to protect the people inside, ironically the person who survives a terrible IED blast is often the one who is the most exposed. The turret gunner, who stands in the middle of the hummvee, gets thrown from the truck and lives while everyone "safely" enclosed by the armor gets trapped inside with the fire and ricocheting shrapnel.

IEDs were a terrible weapon because there wasn't someone to shoot at even if we thought the culprit was nearby. When we were fighting with the laws of war against an enemy who didn't abide by the same laws, complicated rules arose that can be very confusing. It almost seemed as though the rules we enforced on ourselves hurt more than helped us.

ROEs, EOFs, and SOPs

In June 2006, we had been sent to the desert to dig in a sniper hide and watch old ammo dumps. A sniper hide involves digging a fighting hole to fit five or six Marines with their 100 lb packs and equipment. It will usually be chest deep if time permits and have a little hole for human waste. Sometimes it was necessary to take the waste out with us, to leave no trace. The hole wasn't comfortable, but it did the job.

In our case, we were going to be dropped off by 7-ton trucks (called so because of the amount of weight they can carry). We would walk the remaining few clicks and dig in to watch a few abandoned buildings. Digging a sniper hide can take three or four hours depending on the soil or sand subsurface. We had pick-axes and shovels, tan canvas and poles to cover the top of the hole, and enough water, ammo, and batteries for three days.

The private security company, Blackwater, had been guarding this area and pulled out due to contract negotiations. Coalition forces wanted to watch for insurgents who must be interested or curious about the area. The deal was to watch for three days without killing, then after determining a pattern of movement, open fire on guilty parties. Another platoon would creep in behind us and either occupy our holes for the following three days or dig their own.

There were three teams, including my own, in the trucks as they made their way through the desert. The trucks paused and let out each team at their insertion point. No one talked as we sat crammed in the back of the 7-tons. There isn't much room to move about the steel benches and armored walls. Sweat dripped off our heads as we watched the teams jump out the back.

Occasionally the trucks stopped and let out no teams to throw off any enemy who was following our movement. This decoy is called a dummy drop. My team was last, and we were dropped off close to 0230 in the wrong spot.

A Pointman's first job after being dropped off is to move off the road and/or into cover. During the entire truck ride, Lacourse had been watching his compass turn and spin so when he hit the ground, he knew exactly which way to go. As we grabbed our heavy rucks and seated them on our backs, Lacourse was dashing off the road and up the first hill.

Under cover of darkness, Lacourse navigated the terrain to our desired location. This movement took about an hour and a half leaving us at 0400 with an hour or so before sun up and no hole.

Holes can only be dug by two or three people at a time because the other two or three need to be on security. As the hole gets deeper, digging becomes crowded and only one or two can dig effectively. Digging can be slow going and we decided to abandon the whole idea. We would never get our hole dug, fully camouflaged, and security set up before the sun came up. If someone hadn't seen us move in, they would certainly see us standing around digging. Instead, we occupied one of the abandoned buildings facing the way we wanted.

Unfortunately, the buildings in the area were hangars with giant doors on one side. The doors forced us to look in only one direction. We were compelled to cluster on each side of the massive doors and peek out in opposite directions of each other while our rear was unknown. When the sun was up, we were stuck on our respective side of the door with no way of passing over to the other side without being seen. Furthermore, the building was essentially a giant sheet metal Dutch oven and it quickly got toasty inside. Couple all this with the bats that had made the place their home and defecated all over the inside, and it wasn't the most ideal sniper hide.

We saw a few armed people walking around some of the adjacent buildings with rifles and poking around some of the rubble. They drove in and drove off without any apparent knowledge of our whereabouts and we resisted the urge to engage them. Our rules of engagement were clear.

Rules of engagement are the legal way of ensuring all the right people get shot and minimal collateral damage is done in the meantime. Rules of engagement (or more commonly known as ROEs) are explicitly briefed before every mission. Specific ROEs can be assigned to a particular mission but there are always common ROEs for every deployment. ROEs are constantly adapting and changing to the enemy and their tactics.

For instance, let us say mortars begin falling on our position. Mortars are a long-range, indirect-fire weapon requiring someone on the ground telling the mortar team whether they need to fire farther or shorter, more left or more right.

Now let us say we've seen someone with a head wrap talking on a cell phone as the mortars land. We can't attack the mortar team as they are probably too far and will get away by the time we pack up. Yet, we can't attack the person on the phone as we can't prove that he is the reason for the accurate fire.

Simultaneously, we can't prove guilt if he were also holding a GPS. In any educated mind, we would reason that this man is the observer for the mortar rounds, but legally he has done nothing wrong yet – we can't prove he is talking to the mortar team without intercepting his call. This adaptation in ROEs is completely different from the ROEs used during the battle of Fallujah when the rules were, if it moves, shoot it.

ROEs represent the red tape that prevents troops from acting quickly and decisively, and yet they also provide a measure of clarity when the adrenaline and emotions can cloud judgment. The rules are the leash on an aggressive, attack dog. The dog will probably attack all the burglars, but he will probably also attack the neighborhood children if he were unleashed. It is a catch-22; the dog is less effective leashed, but safer to the general public if he is.

During my first deployment, all units had to undergo ROE training each month. 2nd Recon Bn gathered at the chapel, which also served as the site for memorial services and a central point for large meetings such as this one. An officer briefed us on the current threats and adapting problems in Iraq as well as new ROEs and existing ones. We were given "what-if" scenarios and talked them out as well as real scenarios that had happened such as the sniper situation involving the man with the buckets past curfew from the previous chapter.

One very important ROE which was crucial to every operation was our Escalation of Force or EOF measures. Escalation of Force is also used today by law enforcement personnel and ensures a clear message of intent is being understood by the surrounding people.

In our case, the most common EOF situation occurred from our vehicles. Whether we were stationary or moving, there were five steps to follow in an ideal situation.

(1) If a vehicle approached our convoy and we were able to see them far enough away, the gunner, whose torso sticks out the roof of the vehicle, began waving his arms and/or waving a bright orange and pink flag to get the driver's attention. If it was at night, a flashlight or spotlight was used.

(2) If the vehicle didn't stop, each gunner had flares or pop-ups handy. Originally, we shot these directly at the vehicle but we found that they could cause fires in the fields at the side of road. On the other hand, shooting them directly up and out of the offending driver's line of sight was no good. It was up to the gunner's discretion.

(3) If the vehicle still continued, the gunner would pull his M4 rifle from beside him. Turret gunners always had a few tracer rounds in the top of the magazine. Tracer rounds are bullets that light up red and are very visible. He waited a few seconds and then began shooting at the ground in front of the vehicle. If the turret had an M240g 7.62mm machine gun, this step could be done with the machine gun.

(4) The last two steps could be considered one step. The gunner dropped the M4, determining that the driver wasn't going to stop, and grabbed the crew-served machine gun locked in front of him. This weapon was either the M2 (said ma-deuce) .50 cal machine gun or the M240g. The gunner began shooting at the vehicle's grill to disable the car or truck.

(5) The final step was to shoot at the driver himself, but due to kickback of the machine gun and the forward movement of the car, the bullets usually traced upward past the grill into the car anyway.

The expression for these last three steps was "ground-grill-grape", grape affectionately referring to a person's head. We also had an automatic grenade launcher in the turrets called the Mk-19 (said mark-19). Unfortunately, this weapon was ineffective at slowing a vehicle down without completely destroying it and the driver. For this reason, Mk-19s were never used on the lead or trailing vehicle where EOF procedures were likely to occur.

This five step process ensured that if there was a clueless idiot behind the wheel, we gave him enough warning to see us and stop his vehicle. Often times we had someone not respond to the waving or flags and a pop-up was required. Usually this step was as far as it innocently went.

On one particular mission, we were leaving Camp Fallujah to the north and about to make a left onto the main road used by civilians. When we drove in Iraq, we moved all vehicles and traffic to the side of the road. No one drove next to us or near us and if any vehicles got close behind or in front, we began our EOF.

In this case, traffic was trying to move right to left before we could pass so they wouldn't get stuck behind the U.S. convoy. As we got closer and closer, our lead gunner got to the point where he was no longer comfortable with traffic still moving in front of him. He decided to shoot a pop-up at the traffic.

The pop-up spiraled through the air and disappeared inside the front, driver-side window of a car trying to cut in front of us. I was in the turret of the second truck and I yelled incredulously at the gunner, "Did that make it inside?"

Immediately the car halted, the doors flew open and people dashed from the vehicle, fleeing the flames on the inside. The flare had caught the interior on fire! We stopped our convoy and Berg assisted the people with any burns or bruises they had. At the end of the day, it was a lesson well learned on everyone's part; don't try and cut off coalition forces, and we'll try not to shoot a flare into the car from 100+ yards out.

ROEs are always changing and adapting to suit the enemy's tactics. For example, secondary IEDs forced us to stop approaching the downed vehicle on foot. We adopted different methods that involved driving up with a second vehicle or waiting for the downed vehicle to attempt to communicate for a set period of time. Anytime the vehicles stopped, we conducted fives and twenties. Fives and twenties meant scanning the area around your vehicle for five yards and twenty yards for secondary IEDs then getting back inside the armor.

IED emplacements, enemy ambushes or complex attacks, and any other new development in Iraq would bring about new ROEs and Standard Operating Procedures. Standard Operating Procedures, more commonly known as SOPs, were the rules that each unit followed to get the job done. They differ from ROEs in the sense that ROEs are the rules established to uphold the law, whereas SOPs are the rules established to keep people safe.

There were several SOPs that were common to all units and mandated from the top such as the requirement to wear Kevlar sleeves as a turret gunner. If a weak IED went off, the interior of the vehicle remained safe, but the shrapnel could still hurt the gunner who stood exposed. The Kevlar sleeves were to protect against shrapnel and were in line with the U.S. thoughts that if people were getting killed, more armor was the answer. The armor slowed us down, and in the case of the Kevlar sleeves, made us hotter in an already sweltering environment.

Posted high in the briefing room of the Recon HQ was another SOP listing the three Ps we were to follow: be Polite, be Professional, and be Prepared to kill everyone you meet. It seemed humorous and maybe a bit barbaric to some, but it made perfect sense.

The enemy no longer wore uniforms and fought us on a field of battle. It made more sense for them to emplace booby traps, sneak in from behind, and wear whatever blended them in with their surroundings. We had to positively identify any enemy with a weapon before engaging them. Therefore, if the terrorists could inflict casualties without picking up a weapon, they could win the war. We never knew if the person we were breaking bread with was actually the person who emplaced the IED in the road. Unless we saw him explicitly do it, we couldn't do anything about it.

But SOPs were also specific to a unit or a platoon within a unit. An SOP for engineers may not work for a Recon platoon based on the different equipment and training. So SOPs, ROEs, and EOFs need to be tailored for each area, each enemy, and each unit. No one was ever happy about a rule that checked our judgment or forced us to think for a few seconds longer about the guilt of the person in front of us. But in the long run, it saved innocent lives, hopefully without the cost of American ones.

Locals and Terrorists

In the case of the insurgents in Iraq, the terrorists weren't necessarily local to a tribe or village, or even the country. They were just more local than we were. We would drive up and wave to everyone we saw and receive waves in return. But 15 minutes later those same people might be shooting at us or digging in the road to put in an IED.

It was exceedingly frustrating when an IED went off outside a house and the following conversation with the house owner took place:

"Haji, do you know who emplaced the IED outside your house?"

"IED? Outside my house?" replies the Iraqi, confused and scared.

"Yes, Haji. The bomb that was outside your house; did you see anyone putting it in the ground?"

"I don't know of any bomb that is outside my house."

"Didn't you just hear that massive explosion three minutes ago that blew out your windows?" gasps an exasperated Marine.

"Oh. THAT bomb. No, I don't know who did that."

This conversation could be an endless circle of questions with each one being denied until proven otherwise. There isn't an IED until it goes off. The owner doesn't know who did it until they are shown who it is. Unfortunately, this logic doesn't mean the owner doesn't know who did it. He may just be afraid to tell us because of an insurgent stronghold in the area or because we will leave in two years and the insurgents will be around for another two decades.

The term "Haji" can sometimes be seen as an offensive phrase referring to a person of Arabic descent. However, it is also an expression used to describe someone who has made the journey to Mecca and denotes an air of respect. By referring to a man as Haji, or a woman as Hajia, we are elevating them to a respectful status, much like calling someone "doctor" in our culture.

When we first rolled into Iraq and began working consistently in the Zaidon, the insurgents decapitated three men who had talked to us as a warning to the others. It didn't matter how much money we threw at them to fix their house or the water pump, the insurgents had gotten their attention.

To win the war in Iraq, we needed the locals' help. Not because they had any particular skills or assets that we were desperate for, but simply because they recognized everyone in the neighborhood. In the rural areas where I was working, people were born, raised, and married in the same villages. The next door neighbor was an uncle; across the street was a sister and husband; behind the house lived the parents. If a stranger rolled through a village, he'd be as foreign as a white man in a Maasai village.

The trick was convincing the locals that we were there to help. If they told us where the outsiders were, we could remove them and the area would be safe again. But the Iraqis had lived under a fear dictatorship for so long they understood fear more than freedom.

This fear permeated a lot of the countries in the Middle East. In the beginning of 2011, first Tunisia, then Egypt, Jordan, Iran, Libya, and a host of other countries in North Africa and Southwest Asia began to overthrow their dictators. As more protestors boldly stood up for their humanitarian rights, other countries began to see through the cloud of fear that had oppressed them for so long, and shrugged off the mantle of tyranny.

Our interpreter often spent the first few minutes of every conversation explaining to the villagers that they could say whatever they wanted and we wouldn't punish them. We would ask them how they felt about the Americans in the area and the initial answer was always, "Good! I like them." After understanding our "freedom of speech" some were not as happy as they were a second ago.

A few Iraqis explained to us that wherever we went, the insurgents attacked. This reaction endangered their lives and their children. If we left, they believed the insurgents would leave as well. However, villages empty of coalition forces were places for the insurgents to store weapons even if they were mostly safe from firefights.

Here is Iraqi Culture 101: Iraq is broken into three main groups and these groups are further divided into tribes. The three groups are the Sunnis (Soon-ees), Shiites (Shee-ites), and Kurds. The Sunni and Shia refer to different religious sects and are blurred by politics. The Sunni believe that when the prophet Muhammad died, an elected candidate should have replaced him. The Shia believes that a member of Muhammad's family should have succeeded the prophet.

The Sunnis are the powerful upper class group in the Middle East who Saddam kept in power through domination of the Shia. However, Sunni Arabs represent a smaller fraction than the Shiites with the Shiites being the majority in Iraq. However, the Shia forms the lower and middle class which gives the Sunni power.

The Kurds are an ethnicity but still represent a separate group. They are a minority in Iraq as well, inhabiting the north where the oil is. No one likes the Kurds, including Turkey, due to a long history of border dispute after the Ottoman Empire collapsed. One of the crimes Saddam was convicted for was the genocide of his Kurdish people. If Kurds get power anywhere, countries fear that the revolution will draw other Kurds and start a powerful uprising.

Unfortunately, Sunni and Shia don't like each other at all either. I remember standing at an Iraqi police station during my second deployment with a Sunni, who said he just wanted to sweep into Baghdad and kill all the Shiite and then onto Iran. Similarly, my interpreter said, "The Shiites we met in these villages would kill me if they knew I was Sunni."

My interpreter asked me about coming to America and wondered if there would be racism there against him. I explained that there is racism everywhere in the world but he could find an area in America that was Muslim-friendly. He looked at me and began saying that in Iraq there is not as much racism as there appeared to be in America. Yet in the same breath, he would kill an Israeli if he saw him for no other reason than his nationality. I explained that I was part Jewish myself and this shocked him. He had unwittingly befriended an "enemy."

Understanding centuries of struggle, difficulty, and grudges is the primary difficulty in Iraq. We came in with our freedom speeches and democracy ideas and expected everyone to pick up a shovel and pitch in with hard work. But the American fast track to success was not going to take the same path without the same exact circumstances. Even if it did, Iraq would have to endure a revolutionary war, civil war, and slavery, amongst a whole host of other terrible things to mimic America's culture and history.

The problem lies with the three way split. People live in their neighborhood and life goes on as it always did. If they keep to themselves and keep their mouths shut, they are left alone. Some locals during our interviews spoke up and said they liked the freedoms we addressed. Others said they liked Saddam in power because even though they were afraid, things had an order.

I'm not much of a political or history guru. A lot of the culture I learned was local to the area I worked in during my first deployment. We worked in a rural area south of Fallujah that was mostly farmland north of the Euphrates River. We stayed in one area and worked with the same people so I have one perspective on Iraq.

In this area, men did the talking, and women stayed buttoned-up in their burkas. When we went into a house, we made sure we avoided getting too close to the women and avoided eye contact. We wanted to respect the man of the household and if he thought we were ogling his wives, we would get no help from him.

Ninety-nine percent of all the older males I saw wore a long night-shirt looking outfit. This shirt was similar to a long-sleeved shirt but came all the way to the ankles. Underneath, the men wore pants and a t-shirt or maybe a button-up shirt. Some younger men wore western clothing.

This dress was a typical Iraqi dress but we were told women in Baghdad walked around in jeans and western clothing. My second interpreter said that what turned him on about his fiancé was when she showed her wrists and ankles. I can only imagine what he would think about the beaches in Miami.

When we went on knock and talks or entered a house peacefully, we wanted to corral the women into one area without talking to them for safety's sake. We would accomplish this task by pointing absently to no one in particular while using the word for woman. We posted a Marine on the room but he would only occasionally look in to make sure they were all okay and not trying anything funny.

Avoiding women was a difficult ROE to follow. We had received reports that women had smuggled contraband on their bodies but without hugely offending them, we couldn't search them or watch them closely. Recon is a combat unit, and therefore entirely male, so we had no women to help diffuse the situation. We had to often gamble that the women were clean.

The men did most of the talking during knock and talks. This type of patrol involved getting to know the area and the people when we moved in. We talked with each house owner and often

An Iraqi market place during my first deployment

Palm trees and green grass in the Zaidon

times the neighbors would stop in to chat as well so we ended up talking to the same people eight different times.

We asked the men simple information such as work experience, age, tribe, family members, and information like that. But we always got around to the dead end questions such as, "Where are the IEDs?" or "Are there any terrorists in the area?" The answers to these were often, "I don't know."

On one of our patrols, the man of the house said he knew of none of these things. Suddenly, one of his wives came rushing out and chattering to us saying she knew where they were and she could show us! Women aren't any more stupid, clueless, or ignorant of what is going on in Iraq than they are in America. We just had no open invitation to talk to them. On occasion, if the women wanted to tell us something, they were a wealth of information, pent up and ready to help.

There was a trick we used to gauge the friendliness of an area when we initially moved in. We assessed the area's helpfulness by waving to the very young children. If none of the children wanted our candy or refused to wave back at us, it was likely that their heads were filled with anti-American ideas from their parents. If they were all eager to walk right up to the hummvee and touch our ammo and gear, then they were clearly not afraid of us and hadn't been told we were the devil incarnate.

When I came home to the States and visited schools to talk about my deployments, a common question from students was, "What do kids do over there for fun?" I can only speak for the area I worked in, but only wealthy families had working television and steady electricity. Most children had deflated soccer balls they weren't playing with. Troops handed out balls with no air pump.

The most common chore for children in the Zaidon was tending to herds of sheep with sticks or chasing cows that had escaped from their tethers. If the house had a farm with crops, then the women would gather the crop with help from the children and the family donkey.

Of course, when we would roll into town, it was difficult to see what would happen on a regular day as Recon usually went into areas where U.S. forces hadn't been for a while. The lack of troops in the area meant Iraqis rushed out to meet us and talk. The candy we passed out fascinated them with its bright colors and strange packaging. Many people couldn't figure out how to open M&M packets or jolly ranchers! I remember one little boy cradling his

A view of Iraq from a CH-46

A sandstorm several miles away and closing fast

share of M&Ms in his hands and peeking at them every few minutes to laugh at the bright orange, blue, and yellow pieces of chocolate.

The houses were made out of bricks that were baked in the oppressive, dry heat. A lot of the houses shared the same floor plan. Right off the front door was a long rectangular room that we held some of the interviews in. It was the religious prayer room of the house. Most houses were one story, with stairs leading up to the flat roof. The roof sometimes had a three foot wall around the border which we used for security.

The toilet was either inside or outside the house but rarely had running water. The toilet was a pear-shaped bowl sunken in the floor. People did his or her business then with the pitcher of water brought along, washed it down the hole. We never abused the Iraqi's hospitality or ruined any of their things. In fact, we brought our own portable toilet with WAG bags (Waste Alleviating Gel) and we'd reuse our water bottles to pee in. We just had to be careful not to confuse 7-up with piss. We'd burn the waste in a pit outside the house.

There was not always a bed in each house either. Most of the time, the males slept in one room, and the women in another. They slept on thin mats similar to the thickness of a seat cushion and as long as a regular mattress. During the day, they piled these mats above a low chest of drawers. This chest of drawers with the mats was strangely in every single house, without fail.

Rarely did houses have air conditioning, but if they did have a unit, the power was usually out anyway. Sometimes there was a ceiling fan and Marines would try and cluster underneath it to sleep. After I got down from rooftop after 4 hours in the blazing sun, the power usually went out in the village; par for the course.

Dogs are a common occurrence as well – a very common occurrence. Some dogs limped around on three legs as a result of IED blasts or the kids throwing rocks at them. The dogs were everywhere, breeding at will. They barked at everything and ran in packs at night. I often came across dogs with sore throats, continually barking and barking and barking and barking.

During patrols, we kept a close eye on them as they ran up to us. Most would run up and stay a few feet away growling and barking but occasionally one would venture too close for comfort and we would put it down, calling over the radio, "Hush puppy" to let the others know why we had fired. The dogs also tended to attack the military working dogs. The wild dogs had no hesitation in trying to attack this newcomer and we protected our furry Marines.

Between the dogs, chickens, heat, missions and security, and the minuet prayers, it was difficult to get any sleep during the designated four hour sleep period. Just when I started to drift off, the Muslim prayers would begin chanting from the local minuet. These towers were numerous and despite how rundown an area looked, it always had a mosque that sang the prayers more punctually than a GPS could keep time.

After returning from the field one day, I met up with my friend Bailey whom I had met in SOI. It had been an excruciatingly hot week and walking back to our trailers he turned to me and asked, "Vandekar, do you think Iraq would be a nice place to visit?"

Being snarky, I responded, "Well there is that whole problem with the war and people trying to kill us, so..."

"No, I mean if there wasn't a war," he interrupted. "If the place wasn't so rundown with bullet holes and IED craters, what would you think? I'm talking about the culture and environment."

I paused and thought about it for a few minutes. We crunched the loose rocks under our feet as we wove through the concrete barriers towards our waiting beds.

"You know what, Bailey? With the tropical weather, the rivers, and the hospitality of the people, I bet Iraq would be very beautiful."

He agreed.

The Bell

We had deployed in March, just as the temperatures started to climb out of winter. With a thermometer on a patrol in August, we recorded a temperature of 144° F. The air was very dry, though the closer we were to the Euphrates River, the air became more humid. The heat was so unbearable it turned out to be another enemy we had to consider. The wind felt like a hot blow dryer on our faces, and we called it Satan's breath.

With the gear and constant patrols, our clothes built up salt crystals from the constant sweat on our shoulders and thighs. We brought coolers with frozen bottles of water, but after a few days they were all lukewarm. We returned from a patrol, put a water bottle in a sock, poured water on the sock, and hung it in the wind to cool. The heat made everything impossible. We couldn't sleep comfortably and no one even dreamed of heating up an MRE.

We stood up on the flat roof with a three-foot wall surrounding the edge. Each of us sat on MRE boxes or old buckets we had found and looked out a different direction, protecting our platoon below us from attack. We had a wall-mounted M240g machine gun, an M32 grenade launcher and an M40 sniper rifle up there with us, as well as our regular M4's tricked out with whatever scopes and attachments we preferred. Next to us were binoculars and a diagram of the fields and houses in front of us complete with distances to certain objects.

The tar on the roof melted in the sun as we watched the fields surrounding the house. We were up there for four hours at a time, replaced at the end of our shift by another team. There was usually another team on patrol and part of our job (besides to watch out for attack) was to keep an eye out for them. Rooftop was occasionally shot at and the most exposed to mortar fire. But for hours and hours nothing happened and it was difficult to pass the time.

We stood behind sand bags stacked up on the wall to afford us a little more protection against pot-shots and sniper fire. Sometimes we sandwiched a screen of bullet-proof glass as well. In the middle of the roof was a small square of sandbags, approximately 4' long by 5' wide and 3' high. It was called a "ranger grave" and served as protection in case mortars and shrapnel started to fall.

Up on rooftop we talked about everything and anything to pass the time. In a unit full of men, women were brought up regularly, but other subjects ranged from x-men powers, planetary alignments, religious beliefs, and local fauna. I had a game with myself where I tried not to look at my watch for as long as I could. After what felt like 45 minutes, my curiosity got the better of me and I would look down and inevitably see that only 12 minutes had passed.

When I got up on rooftop, I tried to be the first to replace the team already there. Even though this habit meant I was up there a few minutes longer, it meant I could pick the spot with the most shade or easiest space to cover; maybe even closest to the ranger grave. Also, when that team replaced me in the future, they remembered I was consistently early and relieved me first. When it was 10 minutes prior to the next shift, we sent someone down to wake up the next team.

One day, I was on rooftop towards the end of the deployment with Sherpa and Hammer while the sun baked our skins and tried to suck out every available drop of water we had. It was a futile fight against the sun to stay cool. Hydrate or die. We tried to keep the water bottle we had brought up with us in the shade of our bodies, moving it around our legs as the sun crawled across the sky. I swear, Iraq seemed like it was 2,000 miles closer to the sun than the rest of the Earth.

As we stood up there talking about one thing or another, an enormous explosion crashed through our words, interrupting our boredom. It was about 300 meters on the opposite side of the house where I stood, but still close enough to make my knees bend a little.

Sherpa called the distance and magnetic direction of the impact of the mortar round over the radio in his corner. Hammer and I scanned our sectors aware that the mortar team could be on any side and ready to launch another round.

Suddenly, a popping sound was heard directly in front of me. My spot was facing the main road that the driveway intersected with. My view was choked with palm trees and houses, known as dead space. This dead space meant that there were areas that I could not see behind and therefore, potentially hazardous. The mortar team could be anywhere.

The popping sound that had caught our attention was not unlike a distant pop from a cork coming out of a bottle, but obviously much louder due to its range. We all knew what it signified: a POO site. POO stands for Point Of Origin and refers to the location of a mortar team.

When a mortar is fired, a pop is made when the mortar exits the tube. If the tube is close enough and if there is enough silence hanging in the air, sometimes the Recon team can locate the direction of the POO site. This mortar team was one such case. In the case of the first mortar, we had not heard any initial pop but that could have been because we had not been ready for it.

I knew without looking that the other two had turned towards the POO. My eyes scanned the area in front of me, my mouth slightly open in concentration. It was nearly futile to try and find a mortar team because they were able to shoot from a long distance.

Mortar rounds are lobbed not unlike the arc of a punt kick in football. Because of this trajectory, they afford the mortar team a good stand-off distance between the target and tube, keeping the mortar team relatively safe. Still, I looked in case they had been stupid enough to fire close to us and enable me to see between the trunks of the trees. I also looked for a forward observer.

Mortars require a forward observer because the team cannot see what they are shooting at. Someone near the target tells them over a radio or cell phone where to move the rounds. If we could catch the forward observer, the mortars would be shooting blind and hopefully stop altogether.

In my head, I was already counting, "One thousand, two thousand, three thousand..." Mortar rounds would land anywhere from seven to thirteen seconds after they were shot depending on how high they were fired.

Behind me, I could hear Sherpa picking up the handset for the rooftop radio and calling down to the platoon HQ below again. He was giving them a magnetic direction to where we heard the pop and a rough distance based off of how loud it had been. If another platoon or unit somewhere else had heard that sound and called in a distance and direction, the two vectors could be used to pinpoint the mortar team's location. The more vectors we had, the more accurate we could be in finding them. A team in the field could move to their position and kill them before they had a chance to pack up and run.

When I had gotten to about eight thousand, I began to hear the path of the mortar directly up and in front of me. It's not unlike the sound of a jet passing overhead; that stifled scream of an object passing through the air. As with an airplane, I could follow the sound of the object even if I couldn't see it. As I craned my neck upwards and followed the sound with my eyes, I realized that according to my count, the mortar was about to land. I was looking straight up at this point. I began to worry.

My mind flashed on a million things at once. It was dawning on me that in anywhere from 0.01 – 2 seconds, the mortar was about to land smack dab in the middle of the roof. People inside would be ok, just shaken up. However, the three of us on rooftop didn't stand a chance. As my eyes followed the path of the sound over my head, I found myself looking at my fellow Marines.

We didn't say anything to each other. My mouth still hanging open, my helmet plopped askew on my head, armor hanging off my shoulders and rifle in my hands, I stood there speechless. Hammer's eyes darted towards the ranger grave but we all knew if we had any time to get in there, it would be futile against a direct hit anyway. Nobody moved.

My mind raced over all the people back home. All the people I had left and talked to since I got to Iraq. My parents and brothers, my friends and enemies all flashed before my eyes. I wanted to talk to each of them one more time, tell them something significant. I wanted them to know how I felt about Iraq, about them, and leave them with one more piece of wisdom. How would people remember me?

All of this happened in the span of a few electrical firings of my brain. Fractions of a second passed when I saw everyone I knew and thought of things to say. The sound of the mortar passing overhead faded and disappeared altogether. In my head, somehow I was still counting, "…fourteen thousand, fifteen thousand…"

It started to dawn on me that if this mortar was going to decimate us, it would've done so by now. As that thought entered my head, simultaneously an explosion as loud as the first hit the same side as the first one but a little farther off. I let out my breath in a gasp of relief realizing I had been holding it this entire time. I turned back to my sector and kept looking as Sherpa called in the new impact location.

Hammer still scanned his sector, but moved towards my side and encroached upon my sector as well. Two is one, one is none.

Another pop was heard but the first one had already given us our heart-attack for the day. We heard it pass overhead and land even farther away. I heard Sherpa's pause in communication as he listened to traffic relayed to him. He put the headset down and called to us, "It's Paladins. It's our side. Paladin's are shooting at the enemy mortar team."

I stood there confused, not knowing what Paladins were, besides medieval knights. Hammer laughed in crazy relief and explained to me that Paladins were a long range barrage, like artillery but they were mobile. They had technologically located the enemy mortar team when the enemy had fired on us and returned a volley of their own. Death may have dropped by to visit and kept us on our toes, but no one was to go just yet.

Our presence for the majority of the deployment was overt. We used the firm base missions in order to establish a presence in the area for the bulk of the seven month deployment. We operated our regular patrols while serving as QRF for any units. It was during one of these QRF shifts that 1st platoon got heavily attacked.

They were conducting a night time raid on a known insurgent safe house on the far east of the Zaidon, very close to the outskirts of Baghdad. After the raid was conducted and the platoon began gathering information from the detainees, one of the teams was tasked with searching a building on the edges of the area.

Steshko, the team RTO, searched the first lit up interior room with another Marine, Ellsworth, believing it to be a small house. The rest of the team searched the perimeter for anything unusual. As Steshko checked the small room, he realized there was a doorway to a larger area which remained unlit. Upon an initial inspection, he realized he would need the rest of the team.

As the team entered the entrance room they prepared to breach the inner area in typical Recon fashion: stacked up and ready to roll. Debevoise, Piekos (the TL), and Deal (the SARC) led the stack with Steshko and Ellsworth bringing up the rear.

As the first three crossed the threshold, two machine guns opened up on the team from inside, instantly killing Deal. Piekos dove behind some cover while Debevoise provided suppressing fire, killing one, possibly two insurgents. Steshko and Ellsworth never managed to make it into the room and were pinned down in the initial room by heavy machine gun fire.

"Should I frag?" Ellsworth asked, referring to the idea of throwing a fragmentation grenade inside.

"They could still be alive in there," Steshko yelled above the noise. Ellsworth made the judgment call to throw a smoke grenade. Under the cover of the smoke, Piekos was able to rejoin the rest of the team, while the status of Deal and Debevoise remained unknown.

The rest of the platoon consolidated on the house and entered to recover Deal and Debevoise. Deal's body was rescued first. When they laid Deal down to assess his wounds, the platoon realized they had lost their outstanding SARC. He had been hit many times and several of the wounds were underneath his armor.

As the fight progressed, the platoon was able to recover Debevoise as well. While returning fire, he had been hit along the right side of his body and head. After realizing he was in critical condition, but alive, Steshko rendered first aid with the help of Ellsworth.

The fight continued and my platoon was called to help provide a security perimeter while 1st platoon reestablished authority in the area. After rescuing the Marines from inside the house, we realized that the inner room had appeared empty because the insurgents had been moving inside the walls. An inner wall had been constructed to form a walkway and conceal the movement and position of these men. It was from within this walkway that the insurgents had opened up on the team, and the reason that Steshko had initially believed the room to be empty.

Later that morning, as the sun crept up, a bomb was dropped on the building, leveling it, and killing the rest of the insurgents that remained inside. Two outstanding members of the platoon had been taken out of action by the firefight. Deal, a SARC who had been the life of the company, was irreplaceable. Just the day before, my platoon had met up with his and he had entertained everyone with his sense of humor.

The first patrol of most of the missions was designated as a "knock and talk". A knock and talk attempted to establish rapport as we scoped out the neighborhood. We discerned relationships, jobs, economy, and needs all while looking for abandoned buildings that may be used for terrorist hideouts. After the first introduction meetings, the knock and talks were conducted to gather pertinent information about IEDs, terrorist locations, etc. instead of simple demographics.

It was these dismounted patrols that became so successful to the Reconnaissance mission. It became clear to our unit during the

On a dismounted patrol with PRC-119 radio, side sapi-plates, and plenty of water

California desert training exercise that we were able to move quickly and decisively due to a number of factors: the size of our teams, and the equipment and training each team possessed.

Each team and platoon was small enough to mobilize and move in response to an event so quickly and independently that the enemy was unaccustomed to our reaction times compared to an infantry unit. Secondly, teams of five Marines appeared small but were outfitted with sniper rifles, machine guns, M203 grenade launchers, and the capability to talk to each member via radio. In 2006, other units had one radio for as many as 20 Marines. This small unit cohesion allowed us to hide effectively in small numbers, maintain active communication amongst team members and Command, and ambush with enough force to counter a larger enemy.

A clear example of this took place during a patrol in the initial months of the deployment. We had decided to back up a dismounted patrol with two vehicles, because we were unfamiliar of the Zaidon and its threat. My team was in the hummvees coasting behind another team walking on foot a few hundred meters in front of the trucks.

As I sat in the trucks on the radio, monitoring the communications traffic, the dismounted team moved around a corner of a building in the village. Suddenly, shots were fired and Lacourse roared our trucks around the corner and established security. The men shooting at us quickly realized they hadn't been tangoing with only five Marines on foot, but ten and we had brought heavy machine guns mounted on hummvees.

As we moved up the road, we realized they had abandoned a white sedan in the middle of the street. We rounded up the males who matched the description of the shooters while we waited for QRF to bring a military working dog that was attached to us.

Military working dogs are highly trained "Marines" that are able to work off the leash. When the dog arrived, she moved by herself up to the car and sniffed around. She determined that there was something in the trunk of the car so we sent up two Marines to check it out.

We opened the trunk to find an Iraqi male who had been kidnapped from the east side of Baghdad and brought here to the Zaidon. Because the size of our patrol and the speed at which we countered their attack, we had caught the insurgents by surprise and forced them to abandon the car. We were able to save the man and return him safely to his family.

*A rooftop security-watch with no sandbags
or bullet-proof glass*

The Dutch-oven sniper hide in the desert

While we remained at the house in a particular village, in addition to the daytime patrols, we would send one team at a time on 24-48 hour sniper O.P.s. This team would patrol silently at night to a green hide (in the brush or vegetation) or black hide (another house or structure). Sometimes the team would be watching for enemy movement. Other times, Iraqis who preferred to talk to us at night would meet with us to give us information. Their nosy neighbors would be asleep and wouldn't see them cooperating with U.S. troops.

The other teams in the platoon maintained the daytime patrolling schedule. The overt patrolling gave the appearance that all the teams were located in one place. The insurgents moved to strike against the house with mortars or small arms fire, or moved weapons and supplies out of the area. The key to preventing the insurgents from succeeding in moving weapons or attacking us was the placement of the covert team.

Being covert while other coalition forces were moving around was not always safe though. D'Errico, who had been put into A Co., moved to a house for a sniper O.P. They had been dropped off by amtracks (an armored personnel carrier or APC). As per Recon SOP, the team was dropped off several clicks from their destination and they walked the rest of the way.

While the team sniper and ATL got set up on the roof of the house they had chosen, D'Errico and the rest of the team remained on the second story watching the family, monitoring the radio, and holding security on the stairs. While they were setting up, the amtracks got hit with an IED several hundred meters away on their way out. The APCs began scouring the area for enemy combatants or anyone that could have set off the IED. The unit obviously knew there was a Recon team in the area, but had no idea where the team was.

As D'Errico's sniper peered over the roof, the APCs mistook him for an insurgent, and opened fire with heavy machine guns, grenade launchers, and small arms fire.

D'Errico's sniper was hit in the shoulder and his ATL caught a grazing head wound as he jumped off the roof. Miraculously, his fall was broken by the Iraqi house owner fleeing the scene as well. The team shot a white pop-up to indicate friendly forces but the unit mistook it for a missed RPG and increased fire. D'Errico and his team lay huddled in the house and radioed the unit to get them to stop but because of the noise of the guns, they were unable to be heard.

Across the street, another team had been set to provide overwatch on D'Errico's team. The team was able to run into the street and get the attention of the friendly unit. They stopped their fire but it was a loss for everyone.

D'Errico's team's mission was compromised and they were medevaced out for injuries. The officer of the unit who opened fire on them should have exercised more caution and he was relieved of his command. The sniper who was hit in the shoulder stayed in Iraq but remained inside friendly lines for six weeks to recover. The TL, who only received a grazing head wound, received two days off.

The deployment rolled on as we established routines. We did the occasional raid and sniper mission in remote areas for other units but mostly ran operations out of a firm base in the Zaidon. Marines in the unit were routinely hurt and each time I returned to friendly lines, I scanned the returning faces for my friends.

In Iraq, we are given kill numbers to use over the radio instead of names. When we returned to friendly lines, I never knew if the number called over the radio was Bailey or Steshko or one of my other friends. Whenever we saw one another after an intense mission, we gave each other a big hug.

September came. My platoon had been in Iraq since mid-March. My platoon was lucky enough to say we only had a few people hurt and no one killed. Then, towards the end of the month, we got a mission that would change our lives.

Camp Fallujah had been receiving an increase in mortars and the brass was unhappy. They wanted Recon to go out into the field, locate the mortar team, and take them out. Usually the company sent out all three platoons within several miles of each other. In this case, my platoon would go alone and essentially try to draw out the mortar team like bait. We were told in the afternoon of our evening insertion about the mission. We were also told we would only be out of the wire for two days. It all seemed very rushed.

The operation went routinely enough. We picked a house set back from the road and set up security. We didn't conduct a large number of knock and talks because we were in the area to locate a particular enemy, and after seven months, we knew a lot of the people. We patrolled in shifts to look for any caches or unusual activity.

I was on rooftop and nearing the end of my shift when I heard shots from several hundred yards front of me. It was too far to see, but I reported a distance and direction downstairs to the lieutenant. No other troops were out here so I knew it had to be our guys. I didn't know which team was out but when one of the teams came to replace me on rooftop I'd find out. The first guy from team 3 slowly made his way up. I asked the Marine taking my spot what was wrong and he just shook his head.

On my way down the stairs I asked Sean Manning who was on his way up, "What's going on?"

"Z-man," was all he said.

"What's Z-man? What's wrong with Z-man?" I asked, not putting two and two together yet.

"They got Zimmerman," was his reply.

Team 2 had been out on foot patrol and encountered a reed line obstructing their movement. To their right was the road. Racey (TL) called a halt and passed word around to the team.

"Alright, D-ho and I are going to scout ahead and see if there is a way around the reeds to the left," Racey explained to the rest of the team. "I'd rather not get up on the road, but we may not have a choice."

Racey and Donoho (Pointman) went to the left along the reeds to scout a way around. The other four marines spread themselves out in a 360° and waited. After a few minutes, Racey and D-ho returned to the team. On their way back, they motioned to the others to head up to the road. There was no easy way around the reeds.

At that moment, gunfire erupted from the road, chewing up the ground in front of the huddled Marines. Wilson, the team machine gunner, mentioned afterwards that it sounded like two or three rifles. After diving behind some small cover, the Marines returned fire.

Wilson emptied his first drum of ammo before he got an inevitable jam in the M249 SAW. Conroy, the team RTO, was immediately on the radio calling back to the firm base that they were under attack. As the enemy fire diminished, Conroy called out that Zimmerman had been hit.

D-ho ran over to help with first aid, but Zimmerman had been hit in the head. As they waited for QRF to arrive and drive them to the hospital, the team realized their ATL had been killed.

Chris Zimmerman had said to his team that his only goal was to bring them all home safe. He had constantly been looking out for other Marines and putting himself last. As a former crew chief on a helicopter, he had joined Recon with prior USMC knowledge and fit right in as an ATL. He kept true to his word; his team all returned to the States unscathed.

It would be our first and last casualty of the deployment, only 29 days from going home. It didn't seem fair.

QRF was already out when I came downstairs from rooftop.

I couldn't tell you if they returned or went straight back to the hospital. Gunny asked me to pack up Chris's belongings. Chris was such a neat and orderly Marine that when I walked into his team room, his gear and ruck were already packed. I tied it all together and brought it in to the ROC. The firm base remained silent as each of us reflected on the loss of our friend.

Moments when we questioned our mortality occurred over the deployment. At the very end, we began taking fewer chances as we saw the flight home as a very real possibility. On the very last mission in Iraq, as we all stood outside in a circle smoking cigars, someone inside whistled a tune which eerily resembled an incoming mortar round. We all paused and listened. When we had identified the origin of the whistle, we all laughed, went inside, and joked about the horror of the entire platoon getting killed on the very last mission by a single mortar round.

So many units were being hit by IEDs on the way home that the USMC decided to use helos to fly units back to TQ instead of trucks. It was logistically harder but safer. As we staged at the LZ for the pickup, it began to drizzle for the first time in seven months. The flight to TQ was cancelled and the USMC decided it would be easier to truck us out than wait for another opportunity with the helos.

When night fell, we piled into the back of the 7-ton trucks. Using helos would be safer but we'd have to wait for the weather to clear. Using trucks meant we could leave Iraq sooner, but were more dangerous. I got a little nervous. We had entered Iraq this way, so it was poetic that we would leave in the same fashion. I had expected to fight and blow things up when I arrived. Now I was done. I was exhausted. I just wanted to get home.

The trucks were driven by another unit which made us even more nervous. We had only one magazine of ammunition so we placed our lives in their hands. As my truck moseyed through Fallujah, we suddenly came under machine gun fire. The truck suddenly ground to a halt in the middle of the city.

As we sat in the back of these trucks unable to see over the edge, we had no idea who was firing or how many people may be attacking. We just knew that in a firefight, we wanted to keep moving.

"GO! GO! GO!" we began yelling from the back.

"DON'T STOP MOVING!" someone else screamed.

"WHO'S SHOOTING? WHAT'S GOING ON?!"

We had been instructed to remain in the trucks and allow the unit to fight off an enemy in the event of an attack, but during those moments our adrenaline was pumping. After what felt like minutes, the trucks began crawling again and left the city limits. Even when the trucks pulled into TQ we had no idea if another vehicle had suffered casualties. Fortunately, everyone had been alright.

Our company lost seven Recon Marines during our 2006 deployment. That number doesn't include the attached engineers who patrolled alongside Recon Marines and suffered the same fate. This deployment marked one of the bloodiest Recon deployments since the 1970's.

Losing Chris so late in the deployment gave none of us the satisfaction of a completed mission. It felt like a kick in the crotch after the bell. A few of us volunteered to return to Iraq and skip the MEU in order to revisit these areas. But the chances of finding a killer or getting revenge was impossible. The country had waited until the last possible minute before hitting us where it hurt.

Assuming Responsibility

T he loss of our friends prompted a lot of us to want revenge. Towards the end of the deployment, we were asked whether we wanted to go on a Marine Expeditionary Unit or MEU. A MEU, which serves as the 911 of the U.S., is relatively safe. However, if a MEU is called into action, they can interdict sea pirates, escort Americans stranded in a conflict zone, or even deploy to Iraq and Afghanistan if more troops are needed. On a MEU, Marines stay onboard Navy ships and float around stopping off at countries like Spain and Israel. They spend a lot of time on ship training for emergency situations.

Some people never wanted to go back to Iraq again. Barker, Berg, Lacourse, and D'Errico all opted for the MEU. Donoho, Steshko, Bailey, and I were among the Marines who volunteered to return to the sandbox.

When we reached the States, we began several months of training schools. I had already passed Airborne, Fast Rope course, and Coach's course so I was given a choice of dive school or sniper school. I chose dive because of its versatility in the civilian world.

Dive school takes place in Panama City, FL and was much more difficult than any of the other courses I had taken thus far excluding ARS. It involved finning miles at a time culminating in a ten click swim (6.2 miles), extensive academic class work, as well as regular PT. All of it was graded daily and assessed to see if students would drop. During dive school, we learned to SCUBA as well as use the oxygen re-breathers, called the Dräger. We stayed in cushy hotels and were treated well by the cadre, but the constant pressure to pass each day made the school difficult.

During dive school, we first learned how to SCUBA dive using commercial air tanks in a swimming pool. We learned how to breathe with air underwater, buddy-breath with someone else, and then began learning "hits". Hits involved swimming with our head down on the deep end while pulling ourselves along a mat at the bottom of the pool. Instructors on the surface would swim down and attack us on three different levels; easy, medium, or hard.

An instructor on the surface watched our progress and as the underwater instructors came up to report on us, he would speak into a microphone with an underwater speaker. The microphone enabled us to get feedback on our progress.

Easy hits consisted of taking the air out of our mouth, undoing a strap on the air tanks, and messing up our mask. Medium hits entailed all of the above, plus turning off the air and undoing a second strap. The hard hits involved also tying our regulator air line into a knot, undoing all straps, attempting to steal the tanks, and throwing our mask somewhere in the deep end.

In all cases, we needed to wait for the hit to be over (usually lasting around 30 seconds) and then recover our air through a set of procedures. There was always a safety diver nearby in case we needed air but we were not allowed to use him unless we had attempted to restore our own air first and signaled correctly that we needed it. Because there was more time left over in the 30 seconds during the easy hits, the instructors would knee us, bang us against a wall, and make us feel uncomfortable.

I found the hits to be so funny that while the instructors were kneeing me, I began to laugh. The instructor on the underwater microphone saw the bubbles and said, "Vandekar is laughing at you, instructors! Hit him harder!" The next instructor crossed out my name written on the back of my tanks and wrote "Cocksucker." Needless to say, the next hit wasn't so fun and I had to ask the safety diver for air.

While I swam around on my first day of easy hits, one of the students panicked and started to head for the surface. This action can be fatal because the air at 14 feet underwater expands in the blood vessels as one heads to the surface and can cause an arterial gas embolism which can restrict blood flow to the brain.

As I passed the student, he was pressed up against the side of the pool with three instructors holding him down and a safety diver shoving air into his mouth. He did not pass the school.

After single hits, we did buddy hits which meant swimming alongside another Marine and getting hit simultaneously. We were no longer allowed to use the safety diver for air, but had to ask our buddy instead. The same three levels of hits were experienced again on each of us.

After we finished the SCUBA phase with a 120' dive in the Gulf of Mexico, we learned to dive on the Dräger or Lar-V. This rig is a pure oxygen rebreather. Rebreathers take the air that a person expels and converts it back into breathable air. In most cases, this process involves chemically scrubbing the carbon (C) off of carbon dioxide (CO_2), making oxygen (O_2) again. Tactically, this rig enables divers to produce no bubbles, but due to the high concentrations of O_2, divers cannot descend more than 20 feet.

Earlier during dive school, we had been finning individually on the surface as far as 2,000 meters (~1.25 miles) for time. Now that we had learned to dive, we began swimming this distance underwater at night.

Finning underwater presented new problems. Normally we began finning individually as soon as the instructors said, "Go!" With dive rigs, we swam with a buddy due to the possibility of a diving sickness. The instructors also tethered us with a numbered buoy to monitor our progress on the surface. We were tethered to our buddies as well which meant there were a lot of lines and ropes trailing through the water. We rolled out of the boat, hooked up to our buddy, found an azimuth, descended in the water while untangling the buoy line, and began swimming. I was partnered up with Tim Donoho as my dive buddy.

Donoho had been a cook in New York before joining the USMC. After 9/11, he had procured a waiver and enlisted at 29 years old. He was the tallest Marine in the platoon and one of the hardest. There was no doubt in my mind that he had found his calling in life.

Another issue with swimming underwater was our direction. On the surface, we could simply look up and see where to swim. Underwater, we had no sense of direction. For this reason, we took underwater compasses to navigate the distance. We were allowed one "tactical peek" on the surface.

A tactical peek is when a diver pair needs to get some orientation without giving away their position. In dive school, only one diver per pair was allowed up, only his head was allowed to breach the surface, and only at 1,000 meters.

The diver pair would ascend in the water until a few feet below the surface. Only one person in the pair was being graded so he took the tactical peek. After breaching the surface, he found the dock, judged the distance, and took another heading. Once he had taken his look, he signaled his buddy floating eight feet below him. The buddy began pulling him down using the buddy line and swam towards the bottom.

Conducting tactical peeks meant we had to determine when we had reached 1,000 meters. Just as we had a pace count in ARS for 100 meters, we had a fin count at dive school. We had to know when 1,000 meters was coming up so we knew when to conduct our tactical peek. The fin count calculation was based off of an average time from all our surface fins.

After we took our tactical peek on the surface, we would sink to the bottom and check our oxygen levels on a dial on our rig. Our oxygen tanks sat at the bottom of our chest and were only the size of a football. Because we reused the air we breathed out, we didn't need to continually use air from the tank and the tank could be much smaller than conventional SCUBA tanks.

Each underwater fin was based on time and distance. Not only did we have to be fast, but we had to navigate correctly to hit the dock which represented the finish line. Once we passed the dock on either side, an underwater microphone called us up by buoy number.

We could judge how close we were to the dock by the sound of the underwater microphone. We knew how loud the microphone should be so if we heard other teams being called up we roughly knew how far away we were. We could adjust our course a little if the microphone sounded small. The louder it was, the more accurate we had been.

All this finning got us in shape for the ultimate ten click fin. We were dropped off in a bay and told to swim on a certain heading. Ten clicks away were a set of power lines where the boats were going to pick us up. We tethered ourselves in groups of ten and packed energy bars and nuts in our gear. We were still required to swim with canteens, rifle, camis, six lbs of ammunition and a harness to carry our gear.

Using snorkels, we took off with the lead two Marines navigating. Every 15 to 30 minutes we rotated the front two Marines as they had the most resistance through the water. Safety boats motored nearby, watching our progress. Halfway, they had told us, was an airport and we watched the planes fly over the bay to mark our progress.

Some Marines had rubbed Vaseline on their ankles to prevent blisters. I had not been so smart. Finning is a slow process and because we were so far away from the banks of the bay, it was difficult to judge how far we had gone. No one talked. The only sounds were the lapping of the water in our ears, the hollow breathing in our snorkels and the occasional splash as a fin came out of the water.

Five hours and forty-one minutes later, we were pulled out of the water. Two other groups had completed the swim as well and we had all been within nineteen minutes of each other. On either side of both my ankles, holes oozed blood where blisters had formed, broken, and then worn away at my skin. The inside of my lips and tongue were wrinkled from the constant salt water.

We asked the dive cadre what the point was of making us swim ten clicks in open water. The USMC was in Iraq, we reasoned, a country landlocked and not really in danger of an amphibious insertion. The instructors brought up an interesting point in rebuttal that stuck with me.

As with all training, past and present, standards change and things are taken out or put in. If we had to swim four miles on a mission in the future, and the man next to us had not been required to swim six miles in dive school, we would question his ability to make it the whole way. However, because this standard was still held, we could look at him and know he had swum a longer distance at dive school. We could trust him. In small units, trust is not only crucial, it is necessary.

This point is true of all training. Often times training is conducted in swamps, during rain or snow, at night, with little or no food, and with as many miserable conditions one can impose. While these conditions seem to be a logistical problem, it is in fact part of the training. In a firefight, with just one sleepless night, an MRE in our stomach, and fighting during the day, we can feel confident that the other Recon Marines are ready since they have had it much worse at ARS. I knew that every Recon Marine had gone six nights with no sleep and that the dive Marines had swum six miles. I could count on them and that is one of the most important aspects of combat.

On the other hand, if a Recon Marine fails to pass a school he has been sent to, he is less likely to get sent to the next school on the Pipeline when it arises. Each school has a certain number of spots open and the battalion divvies up these seats to the companies.

The companies in turn split them amongst the platoons, sometimes arranging a dive platoon or jump platoon to have specialty precedence. However, if a Marine fails the school, he's wasted the platoon's spot. Next time the platoon has a sniper seat open, they may overlook him and find someone who's ready.

Being able to persevere under any conditions, sacrificing personal comforts, and accomplishing the mission despite the odds are the forte behind every Recon Marine. As one Recon Marine said to me while it was raining, "We aren't truly happy unless we're miserable." Guendner once said that the best place to sleep or patrol in the woods was in the wettest, most mosquito-ridden bog I could find, because I could guarantee no enemy would stumble upon me and compromise the mission. You will find Recon Marines where no one else wants to be.

All Marines embody an esprit de corps, or loyalty. This comradeship is drilled into us from the history lessons and training in Boot Camp. Recon Marines further exude a confidence in each other and a devotion to the community unfound in other units. The traditions blaze in our hearts and we strive to uphold the tremendous reputations of those who went before us.

I returned from Dive School and found that I had been placed in a new platoon as the senior NCO. A new officer, Captain Albert Flores, had been placed in charge of B Co., 1st Platoon with Gunnery Sergeant Hayes as his platoon sergeant. Because neither had been to Iraq recently, they requested from the company a reliable senior Marine who had been on the last deployment. They got me.

Captain Flores had been an intelligence officer before he joined 2nd Reconnaissance Battalion. He came with an amazing attitude and he took care of his men. Gunny Hayes was a Recon Marine cut from the old stock of hardened veterans. While he hadn't been to Iraq recently, he had plenty of combat deployments. He led by example, keeping his gear squared away, and picking up any slack that he saw, regardless of if it was beneath him or not. These two men were the best examples of leaders I have ever had.

One clear example was when we were conducting live shooting exercises during room clearing techniques. We ran through a cement building shooting at plastic targets. Before we entered the building, we were supposed to throw a live grenade.

I had volunteered to move through the house with Steshko's team and as I stood behind the first man, I pulled out a grenade to throw. Gunny Hayes stood by as the safety officer. Stepping around the first Marine, I lobbed a grenade at the door. The grenade hit the door frame and bounced back to land at our feet.

"FRAG! FRAG! FRAG!" I yelled, simultaneously diving behind a nearby concrete barrier. Marines scattered and after the explosion we checked to make sure everyone was alright. I sheepishly looked towards Gunny for punishment. He simply pulled out another grenade, handed it to me, and said, "Again. 'Frag' sounds like a good nickname for you."

The veterans from the last deployment became the team leaders and assistant team leaders in the platoon. Steshko, Kaliszewski, and Donoho became team leaders while Knipe, Mann, and Richter became assistant team leaders. All six were veterans from Iraq. The rest of the platoon had a few veterans but mostly new graduates from ARS.

We conducted similar training from the first deployment for the second deployment. I had always watched the senior Marines with respect and admiration when I had been a new 0321. They seemed so knowledgeable. Now, as we conducted room clearings and taught about IED threats, we shared everything we could remember from our past experiences. We wanted these young men to return home.

Along with new Recon Marines, we received brand new communication Marines as well. Each Recon platoon is allotted one communication Marine (comm. guy). This Marine trains for the MOS of communication and gets assigned to Recon. He never attends ARS or BRC so typically stays with the Platoon Commander or Platoon Sergeant.

Our comm. guys from my first deployment had been on their second deployment. Most of them were not only proficient in radios, but tactical operations as well. When we formed the platoons for my second deployment, many of these experienced comm. guys moved up to the company command and the platoons were issued brand new comm. guys.

These comm. guys were familiar with the radios but did not know how a Recon team would use them. Radios are a complicated, fickle beast that requires the delicate touch of someone who knows what he's doing. Radio waves have to be encrypted, frequencies have to be synced, and internal software has to be programmed. Sometimes in the field, a Recon Marine will have to make his own antennae with an MRE spoon, some copper wire, and coax cable. The comm. guys attached to the platoon need to know what the Recon teams need so they can get the gear and better assist them in the field.

One of my jobs as a proficient RTO from my first deployment was to train the new comm. guy, who we called Bobo. Throughout the year, I harped on Bobo to keep the gear clean and to get the teams whatever they wanted either by begging, borrowing, or stealing.

Just before we deployed again, we went home again for our 30 day leave period to say goodbye to our families and enjoy some time off. When I returned, Captain Flores pulled me aside.

"Bobo has been hit by a car," he began. I didn't say anything. I didn't know what this meant but I knew from Captain's face that something was awry. "He broke his leg on leave and won't be able to deploy with us to Iraq."

"What are we going to do about a comm. guy?" I asked, realizing all the months of training Bobo had been wasted.

"We're going to get another comm. guy from the company but I don't know when that'll be. For now, plan on being the platoon comm. guy. When the new guy arrives, you'll have to train him on everything all over."

I was pissed. Not only had Bobo been a complete waste of time, but I would have to rehash everything to someone else in the field.

The day to board the buses and begin the trip to Iraq arrived and as we waved goodbye to our families, I don't know who was more nervous; the junior guys who had never been to Iraq and had only our stories, or the senior Marines who knew what to expect and anticipated casualties.

As we stopped in Maine to change planes for the trip to Iraq, an old man with Vietnam ribbons came up to me. He shook my hand, looked me in the eye and said, "Bring 'em home, Sergeant."

Iraq – Round Two

Our second deployment was different from the first in almost every way possible. While we had been in the States, we had no way of knowing what was going on in Iraq or how much it was changing. We prepared and trained for the old experiences and expected a lot of the same trauma.

The first obvious difference was the weather. We deployed in the winter for the second tour and the heat, which before had been so crushing, no longer played a factor in mission length. Previously, we were only able to stay out as long as our supplies lasted, particularly water. In the cold, we drank a lot less and were able to stay out of the wire a lot longer. However, the cold weather also meant we had to carry sleeping bags and warming layers. This type of gear isn't heavy, but bulky. Our rucks and hummvees, which had been full of water before, were stuffed tight with sweaters and fleeces.

The seasons also threw a larger wrench in our plans than I expected. During the summer, there was so little rain and clouds. But during the winter it rained, or rather drizzled, frequently. It even snowed several times. The snow turned the muddy roads into sludge and our trucks often got stuck. Stuck trucks were a huge hazard and made us sitting ducks. We sometimes delayed our insertion based on weather alone.

With the change in time of year came a change in the holidays as well. What we never realized during our first deployment was that we weren't missing many holidays. Girlfriends hadn't broken up with their Marines because the summer is an emotionally calm time of year. However, when we left in October, we missed Thanksgiving, Christmas, Hanukah, New Years, and Valentine's Day. These are all emotionally charged holidays and it played a toll on the unit and the families back home. Marines received letters and phone calls from loved ones struggling to cope with their absence. More Marines walked away upset from the phone center after a recent argument with someone they cared about. Deployments were difficult for everyone.

Our unit operated in a completely different way as well. In the previous deployment, we had held an area of Iraq and conducted similar missions repeatedly to prevent insurgents from using the Zaidon. We became accustomed to roads and dangerous areas. We learned who the people were in the villages. We became familiar with the danger.

During the second deployment, we were in support of the general Marine Corps in Iraq. We traveled far and wide to be an asset to various other units who held ground like we had in the first deployment. These missions led us up north to the border of Syria and far south to the border of Saudi Arabia. Every mission was new and unique. Nothing felt familiar.

Because we were used in so many diverse circumstances, our operating structure for the platoon changed. Taking a firm base and conducting dismounted patrols wouldn't work if the USMC asked us to cover 60 square miles in a few days. We couldn't conduct knock and talks if we were told to remain covert the entire time we were in the field. In the end, we ended up using helicopters, zodiacs, Navy boats, hummvees, and even walking straight into the objective. This deployment was more like the old school reconnaissance.

Before, we would move as a team and remain "alone and unafraid" in a mostly lawless area and wait for the inevitable pot shots and mortars. During the second deployment, we moved as a platoon. Rarely did a team venture out by themselves without the full support of the platoon. We made a larger footprint as a result. However, several missions dictated that we remain mobile, so this nomadic type of unit was necessary.

Not only were the platoons operating more collectively, but the vehicles and equipment had changed as well. During the first deployment we rode in five up-armored hummvees and one high-back hummvee (sort of a pickup style hummvee). Now we were given an MRAP (said emrap). MRAPs had a touch screen intercom, backdoor, cushioned seats, space for four radios – and that just came standard. Another truck we were familiar with, the 7-ton, now came with rollers which were used to defeat pressure sensitive IEDs.

The gear we began using in Iraq was more sophisticated and required more training. It was no longer just a radio that we used to talk with; now it could also hook up to a laptop and send pictures or even connect with F/A-18s and see what they were seeing. We previously communicated with frequency hopping technology that would take 20 minutes to explain but now we used crypto codes on one frequency. We also began scanning Iraqis using biometrics such as irises and fingerprints in order to connect suspected insurgents to the rifles they fired.

The Zaidon had surrendered during the time we had been home. The Sheikh or tribal leader had said he was tired of his people being killed and simply switched sides. The Iraqis set up check points, recruited police and Iraqi Army, and set up police stations. Anyone with a gun and mask in the previous deployment would've quickly been shot on sight. Now people with masks and rifles stood on every corner. We had to double-check when we saw an insurgent that we weren't aiming at police or a few volunteer citizens at a checkpoint. It was disconcerting to see someone helping us who I mentally interpreted as an enemy.

The year before, as part of a team, I had been one of the younger guys in the platoon. There were two rooms that my platoon used for planning and gear; the team room and the office. The team room was a room with all our gear and equipment. There were wooden shelves for each Marine and when we returned from the field, we replaced all our rifles, NVGs, binoculars and other gear to its respective spot. This room is where the teams hung out and passed the time on base.

The office was the room where the missions were planned and acted as the business side of the platoon. Only the team leaders went into this room to get briefings from the Captain or Gunny. As 3rd-in-charge of the platoon, I had been evicted from the team room and took up a spot in the office. It was a different environment hanging out with superiors rather than relaxing with my old friends.

Despite the experience I brought to the platoon, there were still things to learn. I had found and countered dozens of IEDs with my last platoon but I had never been hit by one. I went through seven intense months during my first deployment without a scratch and so naturally, at the age of 21, I believed I was invincible. That mentality changed on the very first mission of the deployment.

On October 19th, 2007, my hummvee began its crawl down a dirt road as ninth in a convoy of thirteen vehicles. Third Platoon was leading the convoy with six trucks, company command was in the seventh truck, and my platoon made up the last six trucks. I was seated behind the driver in the command truck with Captain and two Marines. The gunner, Reams, was a veteran from the previous deployment, and Guenard, the driver, was a new Marine out of ARS.

As part of the leadership in the platoon, I had already been on a mission with the Recon unit that we had replaced. We had conducted a 'right seat ride' which refers to an analogy of sitting in the right seat of a truck while the experienced unit 'drives' a mission from the left seat. The Recon unit exchanged tactics, equipment, and ideas about their deployment with us while we plugged them with questions about what had changed in country.

So despite this mission being the first one of the deployment, Iraq felt familiar and I had already been in the field. As my truck turned onto the dirt road framed by ten foot tall reeds on one side and an eight foot tall berm on the other, I sat quietly listening to the squelch of the radio. "It would be lunacy for an insurgent to attack a thirteen vehicle convoy," I thought, "And completely random to target the ninth vehicle." Plus, I was invincible. The familiar ticks of Iraq began to sync up with my body.

There was no warning when the hummvee was bucked upward by the force of a 25 lb IED. Smoke and dust immediately filled the truck. My arm had been resting on the window sill and when the truck lurched from the explosion, it had gone dead. I thought I had lost it altogether.

I felt in the darkness to find out what remained of my arm and where I needed to put a tourniquet. I felt along my arm with my glove, holding my hand in front of my face every few seconds to look for blood. After ensuring that my arm was intact and free of foreign objects, I checked the others in the vehicle. Guenard was sagging out of the vehicle and I grabbed him to pull him back inside. "I'm okay!" he said. "I'm just trying to close my door."

"Reams, are you okay?" I yelled to the gunner. He had been scrambling out of the turret, but only to get the ammo that had fallen free of the gun, not because of an emergency. Captain waved his hands around to clear the smoke and we gave each other the thumbs up.

My hummvee after the IED blast

Near the border of Syria refueling helicopters

Time seemed to slow down when that initial boom resounded through the hummvee. Each of us, lost in our own tasks and thoughts, quickly found ourselves brought together with a common goal to get out alive. Those initial moments of action took fractions of a second. I remember holding the radio handset and thinking, "There has got to be some way to communicate to the platoon in this hummvee."

As I looked around, my eyes settled on the handset and I realized, "This is it!" My mind felt like it was working like sludge as I brought the handset to my ear and relayed that we were unhurt. I tossed the second handset to Captain who relayed to the company the same information. Gunny and the Company Commander both noted in the brief afterwards that it only took seconds for us to get on the radio and relay that we were alright. For those of us in the vehicle, it seemed to take forever.

"Truck 2 has been hit by an IED. Everyone is okay. We're going to try and drive out of the kill zone." After relaying the information to the platoon, I told the driver to drive, not wanting to be in the same spot if there was a second IED around or an ambush set up. Unbeknownst to us, our engine block was scattered for a couple hundred meters and we were missing our front left wheel. Driving was going to be a problem. When the driver hit the gas, nothing happened.

"We can't move. Our truck is immobile," I called over the radio.

Our truck was stuck, and we had just been hit by an IED. I knew that at any moment a complex ambush with small arms fire and secondary IEDs could be sprung. Someone needed to get out of the vehicle and search for secondary IEDs so we could safely remain in the vehicle.

I volunteered to get out and stepped out of my door only to fall into the crater that was left behind by the blast. I climbed to my feet and ran around the vehicle, looking for secondary IEDs. After a cursory search, we began looking for any insurgents or suspicious people in the area.

There were a few farmers in the fields with sheep and there was a speeding pickup truck fleeing the area. Without any positive identification, we couldn't implicate any of these people and they were too far away to detain. The pickup truck driver may simply have been as afraid as we were and was taking his family safely away.

At the top of the road around a bend was an Iraqi police check point. After we had moved the trucks and called in engineers to search the rest of the road, we began asking them if they had seen

Searching the banks of the Euphrates River

A sniper-hide in Iraq during Christmas 2007

any insurgents emplacing IEDs recently. What we gleaned was that this road was understood by the whole area not to be driven on, simply because everyone knew it had IEDs. The IEDs, furthermore, were two years old so no one had been there in ages.

We found five more pressure sensitive IEDs on that road, all behind our vehicle. The IED we had set off was a pressure plate and yet mysteriously the eight other vehicles in front of us, including a truck with a roller, hadn't set it off. Miraculously, no one was hurt besides a few ringing ears and a destroyed vehicle.

In November, my platoon was sweeping some buildings for stored weapons. The buildings were suspected of being a hideout for terrorists moving through the area. As my platoon swept through the buildings, Captain placed the new SARC and me up on an adjacent rooftop. The house was a unique three-story structure and we cleared our way up to the roof to get a good vantage point.

From my view, there was a reed line directly in front of the house with the buildings in question on the other side. To the left were the hummvees that blocked the road for security. The rest of the platoon would move on foot through the buildings and finish far off to the right at the next road. Doc Ward and I would remain on rooftop to follow the progress, relay building information as the ground team moved, and generally provide overwatch.

As the ground troops continued moving, it became clear that they started losing us on the radio. As they continued clearing the buildings, the communications began to get weaker and I started to worry. I suddenly realized I could not communicate with the trucks or the ground team and I had lost visual as well. Even though I knew the platoon was closeby, as far as I was concerned, I was alone and unafraid with my corpsman.

One of my greatest fears in Iraq during both deployments was getting captured and the successive torture that would take place. I didn't care about dying or getting shot, but I was terrified that I would fall unconscious from a blast and wake up with a sack over my head.

"Alright Doc, listen up. We've got to move right now. We're going to clear our way out of this house and then high tail it to the road with the trucks. Stick right behind me and move quickly but decisively."

Ward and I moved downstairs and paused at the bottom floor. My pulse was racing. We checked outside for ominous vans or pickup trucks, expecting the worst. Seeing nothing out of the ordinary, I gave the signal and we jogged to the road. It was a sight for sore eyes when I finally saw those hummvees and their machine guns standing like an impenetrable fortress at the road.

As the deployment progressed, things started to wind down. We tried to keep the younger Marines from getting complacent, but after weeks with no shots fired or mortars, the missions began to get monotonous. We'd leave the wire, walk around the desert, and return. Had Iraq finally cleaned up? Where was everyone?

In March 2008, two platoons were called north to the border of Syria where an infantry unit had been plagued by IEDs. The grunts had a small forward operating base (FOB) that was not much larger than a McDonald's parking lot. They called us in to set up sniper hides and watch for people emplacing the IEDs.

The FOB was a small outpost with sandy berms for a perimeter. Around the edges, concertina wire had been placed to deter movement. The FOB was located way on the outskirts of the main village so the grunts could see people coming. There were only two hardened structures in the FOB: the ROC for the grunts and some shipping containers as sleeping quarters for the Iraqi Army that stayed there.

We arrived and set up a long tent that would house our cots and gear for the week we planned on staying. We ran our radios out of a small room the grunts gave us that had limited access. The base was maybe 100 meters across at its widest.

The teams picked their hide positions off a map that showed the known locations of consistent IEDs. We would drive our own teams into the area and they had the green light to shoot on any insurgent activity. The teams would remain out of the wire for 48 hours and then rotate back in with the other platoon going out.

The teams were radioing consistently that there was no unusual activity. It was the second day of the O.P.s and we began planning for their extract when the grunt commander came in to let us know that a massive sandstorm was expected in the area.

I had been in several sandstorms during my two deployments. Usually the dust turns the sky red and the storm lasts for a few hours. Afterwards, everything has to be cleaned, but no big deal.

As we watched the storm approaching, we realized this one would be different. A wall of sand slowly crept along the horizon like a scene from a movie. We watched its progress miles away as it blanketed everything in its path.

When it hit us, everything turned black as night. The wind tore down poles in the tent and people retreated inside to breathe. I was in the tent when it hit so I decided to move the 60 meters to the ROC to make sure the teams in the field were OK and that radios were working.

In the darkness, I couldn't see my hand in front of my face. Hummvees had their lights on and I couldn't see them from a few feet away. I decided to turn around and walk with my back towards the wind so I could breathe. My eyes were shut tight. As I began turning, I got disoriented by the lack of visual stimulation. I realized that I had no idea which direction to go and I couldn't hear or see anything but the howl of the wind.

I stumbled in the direction I believed was correct and ran into some concertina wire. After disentangling myself, I realized that there were only two sets of wire on this FOB: the wire on the berm and the wire around the generators. The generators were next to the ROC and I managed to clamber inside.

Everything in the little room was covered in sand. The blackness lasted for only an hour or two but then the red Mars-like phenomenon lasted for the rest of the day. Because of the sand in the air, static electricity was high and the teams reported that their radios were overheating and frying. When I spit, the spit sizzled and fizzed with electricity all the way to the ground.

We couldn't navigate safely to get the teams and they were either out of supplies or close to it. If we ventured out to get them and got hit by an IED, no helos would be able to get up in this weather to med-evac us. It was a tough situation.

Captain made the judgment call to go out and retrieve them. Marines came back with irritated skins and headaches from breathing in all the sand. Steshko walked into the ROC with swollen, puffy, red eyes and his hair turned sandy blonde.

Events like this one raised the adrenaline and kept us on our toes. But the danger was not from insurgents. It seemed the country was throwing itself against us.

At the end of the same month, we were called on another interdiction mission. Coalition forces had pushed the insurgents out of Ramadi and Fallujah and into the desert southwest of the cities. Command believed there was also an IED factory in the desert and wanted two Recon platoons to check it out.

My platoon would ride in CH-46s, Army helos with twin rotors on top. Attached to us were a mixed section of an AH-1 Cobra gunship and a UH-1 Huey. Flying ahead of us were two F/A-18 fighter jets. The idea was for the F/A-18s to fly higher and faster across the desert and spot something out. They would notify the Cobra and Huey who would give it a closer inspection. If it was worth taking a look, the CH-46s would drop us on the ground to check it out. The second platoon would make slower sweeps in hummvees.

It was almost April, about a month before we were supposed to leave. Despite only the single IED attack and a few pot-shots, the hairs on the back of my neck began to stand up. I knew all too well what could happen at this stage in the game.

The F/A-18s spotted a white pickup truck with a tarp covering something in the back on a nearby road and notified the mixed section. As the CH-46s flew nearby, the Cobra performed his own version of an EOF to get the vehicle to stop; the pilot maneuvered the gunship in front of the pickup and lowered to just a few feet off the ground. It was a wild game of chicken as the pickup truck sped right under the skids of the Cobra.

The helicopters gave chase as the pickup left the road and sped into the desert. The CH-46s took over the EOF procedures as they had more fuel than the Cobra and Huey. Flying towards the pickup, the pilot banked the helicopter and climbed in order to send the rotor downwash into the pickup's windows. A miniature sandstorm flew into the windscreen and as we looked down the open ramp, we could see the startled and frightened expressions on the faces in the pickup.

Our pilot did this several times before taking it to the next level. He maneuvered the CH-46 directly over the pickup and released flares. Bright balls of fire shot out both sides of the helicopter and yet the pickup continued to try to get away. The helicopters were more than happy to chase.

The CH-46 escalated the force and flew above and to the side of the truck. The door gunner on the M2 .50 cal machine gun opened up at the ground around the pickup and yet the driver simply changed course and sped off. I couldn't believe that he was going to try and outrun four helicopters.

We radioed back to our command on Camp Fallujah. "Black Flag, this is Raider 1. We have a pickup that is moving at a high rate of speed and refuses to stop. We've flown down to their level, released flares, and fired warning shots. Requesting permission to open fire on the truck."

"Negative, Raider 1. Continue EOF procedures, but do not open fire unless you have positive ID of weapons and hostile intent. Raider 3 is en route to your position," came back the reply.

The helicopters continued to circle, chase, and harass the pickup.

Donoho, sitting across from me, began to stomp his feet and scream, "Let us out! Come on, let us out! We can do this!" The tension and frustration was palpable.

The Cobra needed to refuel and since our CH-46 had been flying the EOF procedures, our pilot decided to fly away to refuel the mixed section and allow the other CH-46 pilot to continue. Our helos had giant fuel bladders inside that the Cobra and Huey used to refuel on the ground.

While my helo was away from the truck, the pickup burst a flat tire and ground to a halt. The tarp in the bed flipped back to reveal two men with AKs and machine guns. Three more jumped out of the cab with RPGs and rifles. The Huey barely let them open fire before it tore apart the truck with its minigun. We dejectedly watched from several miles away as the smoke poured into the sky.

We travelled all over Iraq to support other units. We had turkey meat supplied to us in the field on Thanksgiving during cache sweeps; we conducted sniper hides in the desert on Christmas day; we watched for IED makers up near Syria during a sandstorm; we interdicted pickup trucks with helicopters who were suspected in a terrorist training camp; we swept the banks of the Euphrates river with zodiacs to search for weapons caches; we stayed on an abandoned airfield near the border of Saudi Arabia in an old Iraqi hanger that had holes from the initial "shock and awe" campaign.

Each mission brought a level of excitement and the possibility that we may get into a firefight. We relished this idea and were frustrated each time we returned to the wire with the same ammunition we left with.

As with my first deployment, the time inside the wire grew longer, and the time in the field grew shorter. Each time we went out, we warned the younger Marines about complacency and the possibility that this mission could change their lives. And each time, we returned to our routines on base, as if we hadn't even left.

Routine Trauma

There were seven months in each of my deployments. Each time, we were extended a few weeks but we never knew this fact until the end. In our minds, it was seven months, fourteen paychecks, 29 Sundays, or 210 days. It didn't really matter how we looked at it, time moved at its own pace. The trick was finding a rhythm during the down time.

The beginning of the deployments was always the busiest. There was so much to do. I never knew if it was because other units were testing us out or if our commander wanted to get his feet wet right off the bat. Whatever the case, we would spend two weeks outside the wire for two days in.

The first thing to do upon returning to friendly lines was to offload all the trucks with our gear. We had packed them full of water, ammo, food, and equipment and after a mission they held just ammo, trash, and equipment. We stripped the trucks to the bare bones in order to maintain accountability for all our gear: radios, guns, smoke grenades, ammo, etc. Nothing but the wheels and metal that sat on the chassis remained. Each team had its own truck and each member of the team was responsible for a different section.

We removed all the gear and brought it into our team room where we began cleaning it. During the mission, dust and sand found its way into all the cracks and crevices no matter how many times we cleaned it in the field. Radios, unlike a lot of the other equipment, were shared amongst the teams. One mission I may use a PRC-119F and another mission I may use a PRC-150 with a laptop. So instead of storing the radios in the team room with the other equipment, we turned them back into the comm. guy who checked the serial numbers and condition on each one.

Team gear held priority in the work cleanup. Before we focused on ourselves, we disciplined ourselves to focus on the team equipment cleanliness. If I finished radios first, I helped the machine gunners break apart the M2 and clean the parts. After the team gear was squared away, we cleaned our individual rifles, NVGs, and other personal gear. This stage didn't take long as there were much fewer items to clean.

Finally, after everything was squared away and the gear was clean and staged, we headed to chow. There were two chow halls on Camp Fallujah, and they were open for a few hours for each meal. If we were lucky enough to get back in time for the chow hall to open, we went back to the cans, washed our bodies, shaved our faces, and headed to chow like we had never been out in the field.

Sometimes though, we returned just a few minutes before the chow hall would close. If it was okay with Gunny, we ran to the chow hall and grabbed a bite to eat before tackling our gear. It was on one of these occasions that I was standing in line for eggs at breakfast with an unshaven, stubbly face and filthy camis. I had been in the field for at least a week without a shower and I must've reeked. A Marine staff sergeant (my superior) apparently smelled the sweat and odor wafting off of me and said out of the corner of his mouth, "Devil dog, maybe you should put on some deodorant before you come to breakfast."

I didn't even know what to say to the staff sergeant. I stood there looking at him, which prompted him to turn and look back at me. Taking in my appearance for the first time, he realized I had just returned from the field and quickly walked off. While out in the field, there were no showers or bathrooms to use. We tried to shave the day before we returned to the wire in order to seem mildly presentable but the shave didn't meet any USMC standards by a long shot.

Once we finished cleaning our gear and had been to chow, we returned to the cans to have a much needed shower. However, sometimes we were so exhausted and the white sheets on our beds looked so appealing. We passed out encrusted in the sand from the field. Eight hours later we would wake up and realize that our sheets were brown from the dirt and we could now smell ourselves.

On our days inside the wire, there was not much to do to pass the time. My first deployment can had a TV and DVD player, but there were only a few DVDs anyway. Each day was a task at finding something to do. We weren't in Iraq to have fun, so the time spent in the wire was just in anticipation of the next mission.

Every Marine had their own habits and routines that helped him pass the time. During my second deployment, I became very good friends with Chris Knipe, a Marine from Cape May, NJ.

Knipe had served in Alpha Co. during my first deployment so I hadn't known him very well. He was in the ARS class immediately following mine so I hadn't known him in training. He was very quiet and rarely said more than ten words a day. We are polar opposites in many ways so I don't know how we became friends.

Each morning, I woke up and went to Knipe's can. I quietly stepped in and asked him if he wanted to go to breakfast and for 7 months, the answer was always no. After breakfast, I headed to the office to check for upcoming missions, talk to Captain about any intelligence, or draft an email home. When lunch came, I went back to the cans and roused Knipe.

During the day, Knipe and I filled our time with a very predictable routine. After lunch we went to the gym, followed by the internet center. The internet center on Camp Fallujah was a cluster of 40 to 50 computers. It also housed a dark room for watching movies though most people went in to sleep. Alongside the computers was a bank of telephones that used a prepaid phone system. On the other side of the computers was a wall full of books that anyone could take.

There was always a line for the computers or phones. Every half hour, we walked up and waited in line to sign up for a computer or phone. After 4 or 5 pm, the administrative Marines got off work and filled the internet center, but at night there were only a few people using it. Most of the time, I used the internet for an hour and then used the phone to make a few calls to my family.

After using the internet and phones, Knipe and I made the eight minute walk back to the chow hall for dinner. We inevitably talked about family and friends or philosophies about Life, respect, and whatever else was on our minds.

Most units that conducted missions outside of the wire were walled off to maintain operational security. We were no different. Pictured above our entrance was the Recon Jack to let everyone know who worked inside. Inside the offices were the command center, briefing room, a small Recon gym, the chaplain's office, the armory, our team room and platoon office, and every other administrative task that Recon needed.

Between the two company hallways was a memorial hallway. In this hallway were pictures commemorating each Marine who had served with Recon and given the ultimate sacrifice. Inscribed on the wall above a rifle, boots, and helmet were the words, "All gave some. Some gave all."

Parked nearby the offices, and within our wall, was the hummvee lot. We staged our vehicles by platoon and locked the doors to prevent anyone from tampering with our stuff. The vehicles were mostly empty though.

When I had been a junior Marine, I kept out of the offices if I didn't need to be there. I busied myself with PT, the internet, or movies and stopped by once a day to check if there were any upcoming missions. When I received a more important role as the platoon senior NCO, I ended up spending more of my day there, helping Captain Flores plan missions and organizing the office with Gunny Hayes.

On the other side of the Recon compound was the base store. There was a normal USMC store which had magazines, pillows, gum, movies, headphones and other miscellaneous crap. There was also a Turkish store which had rugs, hookahs (an Arabic smoking pipe, much like a bong), paintings, knives, and other culture related items. Right next to this store was a barber shop which everyone used to keep their hair within regulations.

I rarely visited these areas, as I was out in the field for a majority of my time in Iraq. Plus, a lot of the items I needed were simple things like a place to sleep, and entertainment to occupy my time. I'm able to amuse myself with very little so I didn't feel the need to purchase anything from these stores. But they came in handy over Christmas to send things home.

Every few days, the mail arrived to the battalion. It was dropped off at our compound by the base mail Marines and then sorted by platoon. Mail was a huge motivator and it was always exciting to receive. Every other day, we sent a few Marines to check the mail room to see if there was any new mail. If there was, we rallied a few Marines to help carry the boxes and letters back to the team room where we divvied it up. We usually told the other members of the company that the mail had arrived and helped them out if they had a lot of mail.

Mail, like showering and eating, was one of those things we

*Marines hanging out by the cans,
throwing rocks to pass the time*

*Staging vehicles outside the Recon compound
at Camp Fallujah*

reserved for when we had finished all our other tasks. When we returned from the field, we always knew we had mail so it was tempting not to run and get it immediately. After getting my mail, I sat on my rack and read each letter, and began to formulate a response. I tried to write back to each letter I received though not all Marines have that motivation. It was so much easier to email than to take the time to write down thoughts.

There is an expression, "No atheist in a fox hole" which alludes to the fact that when combat gets bad and people get afraid, people turn to God to redeem them. I found this expression to be the opposite of the case.

When bullets started flying and people began dying, a few Marines turned to me and demanded an explanation as to why God would let these men die. I wasn't going to pretend to interpret the will of God so I didn't have a direct answer. I noticed that in Life, people place their faith in certain things. When I was in Iraq, people slept endless hours or went to the gym several times a day or watched movie after movie. They used these activities to cope with the environment we were in.

Hammer, my machine gunner from the first deployment, had been an experienced combat veteran. He went to the gym a lot and when he wasn't lifting, he was sleeping. He called his bed the horizontal time machine. "You just lie down, activate the time machine and when you wake up, it's usually the next day!" he would say. We had to keep it quiet in our room during random times when we found Hammer time-travelling into tomorrow.

One of my pastimes was making amateur movies with the pictures and clips I took during the deployment. I sat up in my rack with my laptop and used Windows Movie Maker to edit the pictures into short summaries of our deployment. Synced up to music, the movies became very popular amongst the company. I used these movies to unwind. When I had made enough movies about the deployment, I turned to making short comedies and parodies with movie soundtracks.

Each day, we checked the office to make sure there wasn't a mission coming up. If the higher-ups gave us enough warning, we spent a few days getting the vehicles ready to leave the wire. I usually got the radios programmed, checked each team's RTO, and made sure all the batteries were charged and stocked.

We occasionally staged our trucks and were told to wait for a certain period of time before we would leave. When this

*Marines reading books and magazines
in the team room*

*A line of trucks staged to begin a convoy
at the start of a mission*

happened, we were only allowed to go to the chow hall or the offices and someone always had to know where we were. Our trucks were rigged up with machine guns and radios ready to go, so we posted a guard on the trucks to prevent anyone from tampering with our equipment.

The chow halls were excellent on Camp Fallujah. I stayed at Camp TQ for a few weeks conducting sniper missions so I ate at that chow hall as well. We were stationed at several little Forward Operating Bases (FOBs) also but for the most part I stayed at Camp Fallujah.

There was a main food line which varied every day. They served chicken cordon bleu, ravioli, and other great food. There was also a fast food line for hamburgers and hotdogs, an international line that had Indian or Chinese food, a salad line, sandwich line, and fruit bar.

In the fridges around the walls there was soda, V8 drinks, sports drinks like Gatorade, and water. They also served Baskin Robbins ice cream! There were two large TVs on each side that showed sports and the news so we could keep up with what was happening back home. It was definitely the cushy life when we came back to base.

A few times, while we were at TQ, the base got mortared. Everyone began talking and rushing for the exit. The only people left eating were Recon Marines and a few hardened Marines from other units. We nodded to each other and helped ourselves to some more ice cream.

The same thing happened again while I was on the computers in the internet center. Mortars began landing and people scrambled for the exit. When we looked around, no one was waiting for the next half hour so we just stayed on the computers for as long as we wanted; a small benefit to getting mortared.

At the end of the deployments, we were given counseling questions asking us how we felt about the experiences we had gone through. I always understood that complaining about having nightmares or being uncomfortable with guts hanging out of a dead insurgent was weakness. However, a few Marines filled it out honestly and were taken off of missions. Instead of supporting these Marines, we ostracized them for letting us down. We had to fill his position which created more work for us.

At the end of the deployments, we transitioned from our cans over to large communal tents for outbound units. This move allowed the incoming Recon unit to fill our cans with their gear.

The tents were hot and smelly. The tiny rooms for three people may have been cramped but at least they were quiet, even with the occasional artillery barrage. With a large tent full of snoring Marines with different routines, it became impossible to get any rest or privacy.

We had left for Iraq thinking everything would be the same. We had arrived assuming that people were going to die but that in the end, we would prevail. We weren't going to let the insurgents win this round.

But everything had changed.

The deployment passed and while there was the occasional gunfire and IED, it was relatively passive. We never needed any replacements. We wouldn't dream of standing outside a house in the open in 2006, but in 2007 people congregated without armor outside buildings to smoke or go to the bathroom. We had constantly warned and prepared the young Marines leading up to the deployment for the mental and emotional trauma that we felt sure to come. But the greatest task was fighting complacency as weeks passed without attack.

As we finished our missions and turned our gear over to the next Recon unit, we got really antsy to return home. Routines changed. Many Marines laid in the sun during their spare time to erase the uneven tans from our t-shirts. Most people shipped home large boxes full of things they had acquired on deployment. When our mail got stopped we knew we were very close to boarding a plane back to the States.

We waited on Camp Fallujah for the 7-ton ride back to TQ, just like we had a year and a half ago. I had been shot at, blown up, and mortared while in Iraq. Each time I had been over, Iraq's way of life had become my way of life. The trauma had become routine. It would definitely follow us home.

The experiences that occurred trained us to react a certain way. We had been taught to instinctively react instantaneously to certain problems and to certain situations. When we returned home, we'd have to unlearn everything we had fine-tuned.

The revenge we sought from 2006 for our comrades never got fulfilled. We did a lot of good in the 2007 deployment. We caught a number of bad guys and we all came back safely but it felt like a joke.

We had signed up to fight again and we ended up patrolling for seven months without firing our rifles. We had wanted to grit our teeth and jump back into the action, knowing full well how hard and traumatic it would be, but our enemy had vanished. It was worse than failing. We hadn't even been given the opportunity to try.

The bell had sounded for a new round but the opposite corner was empty. The enemy had left us with our frustration. The energy we had summoned to volunteer for re-deployment never found its release. The inability to let go became the biggest casualty of all.

PTSD

When people hear about post-traumatic stress disorder they associate a lot of Hollywood symptoms with it. I'm not a psychologist but from my own personal experience, I have found that there is a lot to learn on this subject simply because it differs based on the experience and also on the person involved.

I think the biggest fallacy arising from PTSD, is how one gets PTSD. The name explains that PTSD is simply stress arising after a traumatic event. What is a traumatic event? This definition is subject to personal opinion. A traumatic event could be a car accident, heart attack, or seeing a dead body. A traumatic event can be anything terrifying and obviously changes from person to person. This ambiguity is why 2 out of 24 Marines could get PTSD from an incident that didn't affect any of the others. It is simply the expectations about a situation and what a person can handle.

One of the important things I learned about PTSD was that it doesn't have to be treated like a disease or, as the name implies, a disorder. When I started thinking about PTSD seriously, I replaced "PTSD" in my mind with "stressed out". So instead of thinking, "I have PTSD," I would think, "I'm stressed out."

My first deployment is when I saw most of the incidents that people associate with wartime traumatic events; blood, guts, dead people, explosions, etc. We came back home and I heard of a few problems with a few Marines but for the most part it seemed we all were doing okay adjusting to civilian life again. What we expected to see in Iraq, we saw.

There were a few strange quirks about being home. Traffic was very fast and very close. Lumps on the sides of the road made me nervous and being in crowds was uncomfortable. Sleeping at night alone was very, very quiet. I had just spent every second of seven months within two steps of another Marine. Now I lay in the darkness with the door closed and heard nothing. However, I didn't have nightmares and I got along relatively fine with my family and friends. I had gotten used to Iraq in seven months, so I figured I could reacquaint myself with America again in the same period or less.

My family approached the subject of PTSD tentatively. They weren't sure how to broach the subject and I didn't realize there was anything to talk about. The firefights and explosions were a part of Iraq and I left it there. There were moments when I felt lonely or upset about Zimmerman's death but I rationalized these feelings as natural after any loss, regardless of if it had been in combat or in a car accident.

During the second deployment, we prepared ourselves mentally for the emotional onslaught we expected. We told the younger guys that someone wasn't going to come back. We got so caught up in the idea that the deployments would be the same. When I came back home after an easy deployment, I carried this energy back with me and it began to seep out into my personal life.

The first quirk I noticed came right after I returned from the second deployment. I began arguing with family members and becoming extremely annoyed by them. I asked the other Marines how they felt after our deployment leave period and the veterans who had been on both deployments said they experienced the same annoyances.

The younger guys who had only experienced a peace-time Iraq said they were okay; it was only the senior guys who were struggling. The difference confused me for a while. Why would these combat hardened veterans who survived hell the first time, struggle so much with a safe peace-keeping deployment? It was because of the built-up tension.

When I talked to the other Marines, I noticed that we had similar problems. We all initially argued with family members and returned to Iraq when we slept. However, I was hesitant to label it PTSD. After all, PTSD meant we were crazy, right? And if one of us admitted to PTSD, the others would laugh at him. We all went through the same experiences, so if I began having nightmares, it would mean I was a weaker Recon Marine. Besides, the nightmares were nothing more than hyperbolic dreams of Iraq.

Another reason I was hesitant to say I had PTSD was because of something called survivor's guilt. There are two kinds of survivor's guilt. The first is when one believes that he or she should have done more to save the lives of those who were lost. I came back safe when others lost limbs and lives. I stood in front of Zimmerman's family and apologized for the loss of their son.

The second kind of survivor's guilt is similar. Why should I be "messed up" when others were in much worse shape? Some Marines wouldn't be able to climb stairs, others relearned to walk, while I walked away physically unscathed. Was I really going to say I had mental wounds? Was there such a thing? It seemed like the equivalent of telling someone I had a muscle ache in my arm, while he had his in a cast.

The wounded Marines who had returned home after only two or three months overseas also felt this guilt. Some have told me that they saw us as heroes because we finished the entire seven months, while they left after only one or two. Amazingly, those of us who returned unscathed saw it completely opposite. We saw the Marines who had been injured as heroes because they had given everything.

Most of my symptoms from PTSD came after I left the USMC. My last deployment finished a month before I ended my contract, so I returned from Iraq and went straight home. I lost all my war brothers and the military life in one swoop and it was hard to adjust (even if I was excited to be out of the USMC). When I returned home, my family and friends began suggesting that I was struggling to adjust to civilian life, even if they weren't calling it PTSD.

I also had trouble owning up to the experiences I had led. I returned to my home town and fell into old habits. I hung out with a lot of the same friends from before the Marine Corps. I was older and more mature but Iraq began to feel like a dream. None of the Marines who went with me were around. People began calling me a veteran and at first, this title seemed too big to fit. Veteran stereotypes were old guys in military fatigues from Vietnam who waited at the Veterans Hospital for medication.

PTSD symptoms range all across the board and I can't say that I know them all. I experienced a few of them at different stages of adjusting and I can't claim to know any of the answers. But a lot of the answers I was receiving from others were really frustrating me. The biggest hurdle was realizing and admitting that I had PTSD; admitting that I was stressed out.

The first thing I noticed, as I alluded to before, was relating and communicating with others. On deployments, we were each responsible for our separate tasks. While we were capable of completing the other tasks in the team, it was the RTO who filled the radios, the machine gunner who cleaned the machine gun, the Pointman who picked the way points, etc. We could trust and rely on each other to do the job required. We were five independent cogs working in the same machine towards the same goal.

Back home, I found it very frustrating how much everyone relied on each other. People would ask if I wanted to go to the grocery store or help fold laundry. Someone would ask me to help pick out a restaurant or lay the table for dinner. It was frustrating when people asked me to help finish simple tasks that could be accomplished by one person. Of course, I understood that sharing these tasks was a form of bonding, but I grew aggravated at what I perceived as dependency and inadequacy.

When my family asked me questions about Iraq, I was never sure about what was appropriate to tell them. In my emails home, I had sheltered them from what we were doing and as far as they were concerned, I handed out chocolate to children. A social worker told me that family members would see me more as whom I was, and less easily as what I had become.

When friends asked at a bar to tell them something about the war, I was unclear about how graphic I should be. On occasion, I opened up and shared a story about a Marine getting blown apart and conversation stopped. People stared at me in awe, unsure of what was appropriate to say to me and I became unsure what was appropriate to say to them. Silence loomed.

I learned that there would never be a suitable time to share these memories. I didn't know how to bring them up, and people felt uncomfortable asking about them, like the memories would cause me pain to retell. Lots of civilians have different view points about war, and I approached questions about Iraq with timidity, testing the person's shock factor to the graphic nature of my stories. Often times the timidity was interpreted as hesitation to share, and the person asking felt uncomfortable asking again.

The main thing that bothered me was the lack of maturity and situational awareness. I would arrange to meet someone at 8:00 so I showed up 15 minutes early. They wouldn't show up till 8:06 which had been drilled into my brain as late. If we were five minutes early to a formation, we were ten minutes late. This sort of tardiness, I was taught, could get people killed.

Sometimes, when a red traffic light changed to a green, I sat there for two seconds before cars began to go forward. The lack of situational awareness seemed unbelievable. Didn't they notice it had changed? Why weren't people on their toes? What were they doing at a red light except waiting for green? I was a sheepdog in a world of mostly sheep. I brought this up with my therapist who taught me that if one puts himself or herself in a certain situation for long enough, the brain will physiologically change to become more efficient in that situation. In my case, she said, the adrenaline had bathed my brain so often in seven months that my reaction times had gotten quicker.

People associate movie-style flashbacks to PTSD. We've all seen the movies when the actor zones out and suddenly he's reliving the scenes from earlier in the movie. Noises muffle and after a few minutes, people are staring at him when he comes back to reality because he hasn't heard anything going on around him. My flashbacks are nothing like the Hollywood ones.

There are two kinds of flashbacks I experience. The first is voluntary. I will get uncomfortable with a situation or argument and I want to retreat. Something around me has made me uncomfortable enough that I want to find a memory in which I was confident. For me, these memories are in Iraq. I begin to pour over memories of throwing on my gear, checking my magazines, loading radio frequencies, and the responsibilities of being in a team. It's this calming confidence in my ability that lets me escape the confrontation I'm currently in. Calling up these memories is not uncomfortable to me, but I don't know if it's considered healthy. I am aware of the situation and my surroundings, but half my mind is elsewhere.

The second flashback happens less often. I've heard it described from a therapist as "hijacking your mind". This flashback occurs when I hear or smell something familiar to a memory and suddenly I am replaying an uncomfortable memory. This flashback can happen to anyone who has had a bad experience with a significant other or a bad play in a big game. The effect the flashback has is directly related to how important the memory was, regardless of what happened during the event. It can really mess one up when the memory being replayed cost lives or touched on the edge of death. These memories are the ones that make me cringe.

Contrary to movie-style flashbacks though, I'm aware of what's going on around me, and I can function normally. My mind is off somewhere else wishing I had taken a few more minutes to check my gear or cringing at an image but I am able to pay the cashier, write a paper, or whatever is in front of me

I have a hard time pulling my mind back from these hijacking memories as they replay in my head over and over. They are strong enough to alter my mood and my wife has been attentive to notice when they begin to happen without me saying anything.

All in all, the memories that resurface the most about Iraq are the little details that occurred every day we were over there: standing around a burn pit, sitting down to take notes on a conversation, or the weight of my gear sitting on my shoulders. These memories don't affect me in any way. College graduates think about university in the same way. Iraq was a significant part of my life and I will always remember, but it's over.

Another symptom that people associate with PTSD is nightmares. When I think of nightmares, I think of a dream that is so horrible that I am in a panic to escape from it. Some type of monster is killing innocent people or terrifying me. My nightmares have subsided and they occur less frequently now. There were two kinds that I can remember: the kind when I was in the thick of the fighting and bodies lay all around me or the kind when I was killing innocent people. In these dreams, I am the monster.

Both of these dreams make me uncomfortable when I wake up but I never wake up in a sweat or leap out of bed. I never felt it was a nightmare. Similar to the flashbacks, I was just reliving things I had already done on an exaggerated scale, so I didn't feel that the memory was all that terrible. The dreams are usually hyperbolic memories. Memories that may have happened but my mind has made it bigger, scarier, or louder. It was only when I talked to people who hadn't been to combat that I learned this kind of dream was unusual.

The biggest setback to my dreams comes from the fact that I talk in my sleep very frequently. As a sleep walker, my wife gets nervous that I will misinterpret her as an enemy. She has woken up to find me sitting up in bed breathing rapidly. When she asked what I was doing, I told her, "We are killing someone. Have we done this before?" In the middle of the night, this can be very eerie.

Overall, the number one moment when I retreated to Iraq in my mind would be when I hung out in crowds. I began to get anxious and felt tightness in my chest resulting from a lack of control over the situation. It wasn't that I was unaware of where I was or that I couldn't separate my Iraq crowd control experiences from the present one. I just felt uncomfortable.

In Iraq, there were always five of us with rifles and radios and even if shit hit the proverbial fan, we had a plan to escape and deal death to those who opposed us. We may have been outnumbered, but we were ready. We were the most dangerous people for hundreds of miles. Now I was in a bar with no backup, no weapon, and no control. It just made me nervous.

As I began to realize and accept that I was struggling with adapting to life outside Recon, I started to look for answers. I began seeing a therapist at the Veterans Association (VA) and telling the people close to me about my experiences. The therapist didn't last long because I didn't respect her enough to put time and effort into the meetings.

The therapist also told me that opening up to my family would do more harm than good. She said my family would want to help solve the problem. They would also be the most shocked with the change in my character. Some of the things I would tell them, they would have trouble believing simply because they remembered me from before the USMC.

I did learn that there was no miracle cure that would take all the memories away. I realized that I was looking for some way to be like everyone else. I was looking for a way to "get better." I was looking for a button, a word, a drug, or a thought that would switch off my mind and help me see things the way everyone else did.

On the other hand, I had accomplished so much through the USMC and had learned to see things as a Recon Marine. I had overcome obstacles and my confidence allowed me to believe there wasn't anything I couldn't do. I didn't want to forget the principles I had accepted to become a Recon Marine. Yet my conditioning was hindering me from assimilating easily into civilian life. It was a catch-22. I didn't want to forget but I didn't want to remember.

It was talking to older veterans from Vietnam and Korea that made me realize I would have to learn to live with the differences and memories. Some symptoms would begin to fade, they told me, but others would surface for the first time many years later. I just had to build new memories after the USMC and that would take time. I accepted that there was no miracle cure or confession that would make me "normal." I was going to be a Recon Marine my whole life, and while I was very proud of what I had accomplished, I had to accept that I was always going to be upset by the inadequacy of others around me. This knowledge brought me to another realization.

Post-traumatic stress is a normal reaction to an abnormal situation. If I had gone to Iraq, killed people, seen friends die, and come back as if nothing had changed, that would've been more of a warning sign than if I came back in shock. Having PTSD didn't make me crazy or weak. It meant I was sane.

I started to call the other Marines who had served both deployments and asked them how they were coping. Almost all of them were struggling with civilian life in one aspect or another. Some were treated at the VA, while others treated themselves with drugs and alcohol. One Marine lost himself in a church. Many of them joined private security agencies; a civilian equivalent job to Recon.

While we didn't necessarily miss the USMC rules and formations, it was the band of brotherhood we had lost. We missed being dangerous. We walked around people who had no idea what we had done. We had used millions of dollars in equipment to survive on our own amongst people who wanted to kill us and now we were lifeguards, waiters, students, and clerks. Where was the respect? It should be the combat veterans and Purple Heart recipients who get paid millions to sacrifice their lives, not the actors and athletes. They should make trading cards with military units on the front, not baseball players.

Despite the fact that my flashbacks involved experiences in Iraq, the thing that every Recon Marine misses most is the camaraderie. The esprit de corps that embodies itself into each Marine at Boot Camp is exponentially increased when the same Marines go into combat together. When a group of people go through a hardship, they are brought tighter together. Knowing that each one of us had suffered through RTP, ARS, and Iraq meant we all shared a common bond.

John Rambo, at the end of the popular movie *First Blood*, rants about his PTSD and the struggle to return home from Vietnam and find his place as a killer back in society. He says, "Nothing is over! Nothing! You just don't turn it off!" He mentions that he had been trusted with so much responsibility overseas and now he couldn't even hold a job parking cars. It's this imbalance that frustrates many Recon Marines to go back to what they know. They join police departments, private security firms, reenlist, or become paramedics and firefighters.

At the end of every enlistment, Marines are required to attend separation training. During separation training, Marines learn to write résumés based on their MOS and proper etiquette during an interview. This training is excellent for air conditioning mechanics, truck drivers, and administrative clerks. However, one Recon Marine I went with raised his hand and asked sarcastically, "If all we were taught is how to kill people, how do we put that on our résumé?" While it was a crude and simple explanation of Recon, it summed up the realization that we had learned a lot of skills that were not commonplace outside of the battlefield.

So why didn't I reenlist or join private security? What kept me in school? What grounded me and kept me trying to persevere? When I got out of the USMC, within two months I went hiking through the middle of Italy with D'Errico, the Marine who had joined Boot Camp with me. We had gone through RTP together and shared bunks at ARS. We had been in separate companies in Iraq but we had always maintained our friendship.

While we were in Italy for a month, we slept next to streams and rivers, cooked our food over a fire, and generally had a good time. It was a great trip because it resembled our life in the military without any of the deadlines or haircuts. I was in a foreign country with one of my best friends. It let us keep the good a little longer.

After I got back from Italy, I began dating my wife, Meg MacCart. I had known her for nine years, so she knew who I was before the USMC. I also wrote countless letters to her from Iraq so she had a working knowledge of the military without me having to explain everything. She had recently lost her father and we understood each other on an emotional level.

I left the USMC because I didn't want to deploy when I eventually had a family and I knew I didn't want to make it a career. I wanted to see more of Life. When I struggled with adjusting or nightmares, I called Meg and she listened. She was able to keep me focused on graduating from university, and encouraged me not to join a private security firm. There is nothing wrong with that career path, it just wasn't for me. It represented the easy way out for me, and as a Recon Marine, I couldn't quit.

When I started going to school, I made it a personal goal to graduate with all A's. I set this goal for myself because I felt that I had come back when others had lost their lives in Iraq. I shouldn't be allowed to put only half an effort into something when others had given 100 percent. If I could get an A but achieved a B, I wasn't doing their memory any honor. I had to uphold their tremendous reputation. I dedicated this goal to their memory and it helped me succeed when I could've taken the easy route. I ended up graduating with a 4.0 GPA.

I told my wife that Recon Marines are excellent at adapting, overcoming, and persevering, except when it comes to life outside of Recon. We remain forever Recon, for better or worse.

SitRep

M any Marines that served with me helped me write this book. They are in all phases and walks of life, still discovering who they are and where they fit in. Looking back, it is hard to believe that such young men were capable of achieving so much. They continue to take their Recon background into their future.

Keith Zeier was injured by an IED on July 17th, 2006. The doctors were unsure if he would walk, let alone run, ever again. In 2009, Zeier ran a 100-mile ultra marathon in the Florida Keys to raise money for the Special Operations Wounded Warrior Foundation. He stopped only once to receive an IV and lost 20 lbs. Due to his injury, he was never able to run more than five miles to train for the run. He finished in just over 31 hours. A year later, his leg was amputated.

Joe Lacourse returned to Massachusetts after getting his Master Dive certificate in Florida. He received his paramedic license and joined the local fire department where he serves today.

David D'Errico married and had a young girl. He received his EMT license and deployed to Afghanistan with a private security company. He plans on moving to Indiana with our friend, Josiah Bailey.

Josiah Bailey married his childhood sweetheart with whom he now has four kids. He helps his dad with his log cabin business and works on construction. With D'Errico, his brothers, and some help from me, he built his own house in Indiana.

Chris Brink lives in Melbourne, FL with his wife and son. He is currently working on receiving compensation for the injuries he suffered in Iraq.

Stephen Barker works with a non-profit organization in Colorado teaching snowboarding.

Chris Knipe received his associates' degree and continues to live in Cape May, NJ. He completed his EMT license as well, and is currently enrolled in a university to complete his degree in either medicine or microbiology.

Nick Steshko moved back to Washington D.C. where he married a college sweetheart. He is attending classes to receive his degree and plans on commissioning as an officer, like his father before him.

Tim Donoho left the USMC for a bit. He enjoyed his time outside the USMC and then went into the reserves with 4th Force Recon. In 2010, he voluntarily deployed to Afghanistan and then again in 2011.

Albert Flores went on to command Alpha Co. in Afghanistan. He left the USMC and is planning on going to graduate school in order to pursue Political Science.

John Hayes went with Flores to Afghanistan and served honorably at his side as his operations chief. Master Sergeant Hayes was killed in 2009 by an IED attack. He remains one of my heroes.

Sean Manning left the USMC to attend the University of Connecticut for Mechanical Engineering. He was hired by the Research and Development department of Colt Defense and competed for the company on their shooting team. He recently started work for Sig Sauer doing similar work.

Lynn Westover became a BRC instructor on the west coast after my first deployment. He got married and divorced before being stationed out in Okinawa, Japan where he works with 3rd Recon and continues to deploy.

Chris Berg went to Afghanistan with MarSOC, the new Marine Corps Special Operations Command unit. After leaving the Navy, he got married and became a firefighter at Eagle River Fire Protection District in Colorado. He plans on becoming a helicopter pilot.

I left the USMC and backpacked with D'Errico through Tuscany. After I returned, I spent a few months at home before going back to college to finish my degree. I became a commercial pilot as I had always dreamed and began writing the book you now hold in your hands. Two years after leaving the USMC, I married Meghan MacCart, who I had known for 11 years.

I lost touch with other Marines and many drift in and out with an occasional phone call or email. It is inevitable that we get swept apart. We remain alone and unafraid out in the world. But I know that one day, the fallen Marines and the Marines who carry on the torch will reunite in the halls of Valhalla. Aarugah, snake eaters!

Fair Winds and Following Seas

Acronyms & Explanations

0321	MOSs have four number designators. The first two refer to the general type (03 = infantry). The second two refer to a specific job within that type (0321 = Recon Marine, 0311 = rifleman, etc.)
7-Ton	Massive six-wheeled vehicle that can carry gear or troops. Called 7-ton because of the amount of weight it can carry
8-count	Exercise involving 8 counts in one repetition. 1) Squat 2)pushup position 3) down 4) pushup 5)legs apart 6) legs together 7) squat 8) stand again
Acog	2x optical scope that doesn't require batteries
APC	(Armored Personnel Carrier) Similar to a tank in armor but without a heavy bore gun. Able to transport troops

ARS	(Amphibious Reconnaissance School) Where Marines go to become Recon Marines on the east coast. No longer exists
ARTO	(Assistant Radio Transmission Operator) Helps the RTO with radio procedures
Arty Sim	(Artillery Simulator) Grenade used to simulate incoming artillery strikes. The grenade starts with a whistle and ends with a bang
AT-4	Single shot rocket launcher employed by dismounted troops against armor
ATL	(Assistant Team Leader) Responsible for policing the area a team vacates. 2nd-in-command of the team, who typically enforces the rules set by the TL
Azimuth	Compass direction
BAS	(Battalion Aid Station) Location of the corpsman and sick call
Bn	(Battalion) A battalion is made up of several companies. Several battalions make up a regiment
BRC	(Basic Reconnaissance Course) Where Marines go to become Recon Marines on the west coast
Cadre	Name for the instructors at ARS
Camis	Camouflage uniforms [pronounced kamees]
Cas-evac	(Casualty Evacuation) Helicopter or hummvees that come to take wounded people to the hospital [pronounced kas evak]

Claymore	Directional C4 mine with ball bearings detonated by hand
Click	Kilometer
Co.	(Company) Several platoons make up a company. Several companies make up a battalion
Comm. Guy	Marines deployed with Recon platoons that have the MOS of communication. They specialize in radios and assist Recon teams in establishing voice or data communication
Concertina wire	Similar to barbed wire but with trapezoidal barbs instead of points
Corpsman	Medics trained by the Navy to work in the Marine Corps [pronounced core-mun]
Cpl	(Corporal) Fourth rank in the enlisted USMC, designated as E-4. Also the first non-commissioned officer
CS	Gas used as a riot agent that causes painful chest pains and irritates the eyes and skin. Named for the last name initials of the creators, Ben Corson and Roger Stoughton
CWS	(Combat Water Survival) Four levels of swim qualifications used by the USMC to judge swim proficiency
DI	(Drill Instructor) Instructors for Boot Camp
E&E	(Escape and Evasion) While used in regular missions, also refers to the run at the end of patrol week

Eotech	Sight used on small arms that produces a circle with a dot in the middle. Battery powered with no zoom
FOB	(Forward Operating Base) Semi-permanent small base used by military forces to conduct missions. Can vary enormously based on location but typically has mounted machine gun defenses, reinforced sandbag positions, and enough room to park several hummvees [pronounced fob]
Grunts	Infantry Marines, specifically Marines with the 03xx MOS designator
Gy Sgt	(Gunnery Sergeant) Seventh rank of the enlisted USMC, designated E-7. Referred to as Gunny
Helo	Helicopter
HMMWV	(High Mobility Multiple Wheeled Vehicle) Truck used extensively by the military for many purposes. Typically seats four individuals with a fifth in the turret. Also written hummvee [pronounced hum vee]
HQ	(Headquarters) Any place that operations are run out of, officers collect, or is central to a mission command
HRST	(Helicopter Rope Suspension Technique) Any rope system that involves a helicopter including rappelling out of a helo, SPIE, and fast roping [pronounced herst]
HVI	(High Value Individual) Suspected enemy combatant of interest to HQ. Not to be confused with a Very Important Person (VIP) who is friendly

IED	(Improvised Explosive Device) Any homemade explosive that is rigged outside of commercial means, i.e. C4 stuffed inside a soda can connected to a cell phone, 105mm artillery round connected to pressure switch
LAR	(Light Armored Reconnaissance) Usually referring to the unit by the same name, this unit rides in APCs and accepts a lot of ARS drop outs
Lcpl	(Lance Corporal) Third rank in the enlisted USMC, designated E-3. Jokingly referred to as lance cooley or lance criminal
LZ	(Landing Zone) On Camp Lejeune, these are named after birds and used by units as part of training
M240	7.62mm belt fed machine gun mounted on a hummvee, tripod, or wall. Could be M240g or M240b which refers to minor changes in the gun
M249 SAW	5.56mm belt or magazine fed squad automatic weapon able to be used dismounted
M4	5.56mm magazine fed rifle employed by U.S. troops, similar to the M16
M40	7.62mm bolt-action magazine fed sniper rifle similar to the civilian Remington 700
M9	9mm pistol
MCT	(Marine Combat Training) Training following Boot Camp for all Marines not in the infantry
Med-evac	(Medical Evacuation) See Cas-evac

MEU	(Marine Expeditionary Unit) Marines aboard Navy ships that standby for immediate assistance in any U.S. engagement. They represent America's 911 force [pronounced me-ew]
MOS	(Military Occupational Specialty) Job that each person is assigned to in the military. People can have more than one, and each branch has its own system
MRAP	(Mine Resistant Ambush Protection) Also known as the Cougar. Vehicle designed to counter IEDs with increased armor and effectiveness [pronounced emrap]
MRE	(Meals Ready to Eat) meals designed to provide a balanced meal with increased calorie intake. Also designed to last a long time
NCO	(Non-Commissioned Officers) Represented by corporals and sergeants, these ranks are enlisted members who generally have proved responsible enough to lead Marines
NOD	(Night Optic Device) night vision device that can be monocular or binocular (one or two eyes). Enhances the wearers ability to see light including infrared [pronounced nod]
NVG	(Night Vision Goggle) see NOD
OP	(Observation Post) Any post that requires remaining covert while gathering information on a target or providing overwatch/security on an area
PFC	(Private First Class) Second rank in the enlisted USMC, designated E-2. Jokingly referred to as "Perfect For Cleaning"

PFT	(Physical Fitness Test) USMC standard for fitness generated by a 300 pt score. 100 crunches, 18:00 three mile run, and 20 pull ups is a perfect score
POG	(Person Other than Grunt) Anyone not in the infantry, specifically non-combat units. Typically used in a derogatory fashion [pronounced poh-g]
Police Call	Picking up trash or expended ammunition casings
POO	(Point Of Origin) Location of a mortar site when a mortar is launched. Could also refer to artillery [pronounced poo]
POW	(Prisoners Of War) Combatants that have been captured by the enemy in accordance with the Geneva Conventions
PT	(Physical Training) Any exercise format. Not the same as a PFT in the sense that it has no standard layout
QRF	(Quick Reaction Force) Standby unit of any size that can be mobilized quickly and efficiently to respond to a crisis or emergency
ROC	(Radio Operations Center) Location of centralized command radios. Located within the HQ [pronounced rock]
ROE	(Rules of Engagement) Rules established by a military, unit, or authority to maintain the law
Rollers	Set of many small wheels in front of a truck that are driven into pressure sensitive IEDs in order to set them off

Ropes	Marines at 2nd Reconnaissance Battalion training to join Recon, distinguished by the training ropes worn as a sash
RTO	(Radio Transmission Operator) Member of a team in charge of communications and radios
RTP	(Recon Training Platoon) Unit at 2nd Reconnaissance Battalion training to go to ARS
Ruck	Backpack used by the military. Typically refers to larger packs (smaller packs called daypacks)
S-2	Intelligence branch of any unit
SARC	(Special Amphibious Reconnaissance Corpsman) Corpsmen that have been through ARS or BRC [pronounced sark]
SERE	Survival, Escape, Resistance, Evasion) School designed to train the military on survival techniques and interrogation resistance [pronounced sear]
Sgt	(Sergeant) Fifth rank in the enlisted USMC, designated as E-5. Generally the backbone of the USMC and last rank of the non-commissioned officers
SitRep	(Situation Report) Report over the radio that details the current situation
SOI	(School of Infantry) School for infantry Marines that teaches basic war-fighting tactics, land navigation, and other infantry functions
SOP	(Standard Operations Procedures) Rules established by a military, unit, or authority to maintain safety

SPIE	(Special Person Insert Extract) Technique used to remove troops from areas where helicopters cannot land. Involves hooking individually up to a rope suspended from a helicopter [pronounced spy]
SSgt	(Staff Sergeant) Sixth rank in the enlisted USMC, designated as E-6. First of the staff non-commissioned officers
TL	(Team Leader) Team member responsible for everything the team does or fails to do
TQ	Al-Taqaddum, an air base in Iraq
UAV	(Unmanned Aerial Vehicles) Aircraft piloted by computer or remote control for visual reconnaissance or interdiction purposes
USMC	(United States Marine Corps) Branch of the military, department of the Navy, devoted to securing bases close to the water
VBIED	(Vehicle Borne Improvised Explosive Device) IED emplaced or built in a car or truck solely for the purpose of mobility and detonation within the vehicle [pronounced veebid
WAG Bags	(Waste Alleviation and Gelling bags) Bags used for bathroom use
Zodiac	Inflatable rubber rafts attached to an outboard motor that typically fit six Marines

Special Thanks to:

- My wife, Meghan, for helping me edit the book. She has been patient and thoughtful throughout the process and supported me in every way.
- Dan Winton, Chris Berg, Brian Rogge, Chris Knipe, David D'Errico, Steve Barker, and Joe Lacourse for helping to keep me consistent and accurate. Aarugah, snake-eaters.
- Sean Manning, Nick Steshko, and Sam Wilson for their contributions. Several passages are directly recollected from their memories.
- Laura Tessier, Hunter Barnhill, my dad, mom, and brothers who helped with their honest criticism.
- Joab Lupio and Jonathon Diaz for their amazing cover design and hard work.
- Countless others who helped prod, poke, add, and subtract from this memory in an effort to keep it interesting, concise and accurate.

Shipmates Four by Bert Falardeau

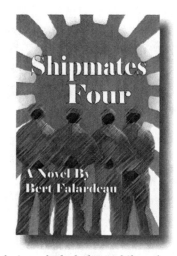

Shipmates Four is the rarest of books, a self-styled novel but with gripping color, anecdotes and descriptions that could only have come from someone actually present when history was made. Bert Falardeau, 84 years young, has captured an era in time that comes alive in his telling of four young sailors and their first taste of sea duty during the years of World War II.

Anyone who has been in the Navy will resonate with the tales and adventures of these shipmates of USS Venus. It is somehow comforting to realize that sailors today and sailors of sixty years ago aboard the good ship Venus share many of the same day-to-day shipboard observations, camaraderie and "deckplate" philosophy. Mr. Falardeau brings this link between generations to life in an attractive format that will resonate with a broad spectrum of readers.

You may order online at www.bluewaterpress.com/shipmates or by mail:

BluewaterPress LLC
52 Tuscan Way Ste 202-309
Saint Augustine FL 32092

Name: _____

Address: _____

City, State, Zip: _____

Phone number: _____

Email Address: _____
(All information kept in the strictest confidence)

Please send me Bert Falardeau's *Shipmates Four.* Cost is $20.95 per copy. Shipping & handling is $3.95 per book for one copy, $6.95 for up to seven of any titles, and $1.15 per book for any combination of more than seven.

Number of books _____ x $20.95 = _____

Shipping and handling = _____

FL residents, please add sales tax for county of residence = _____

Total remitted = _____

We gladly accept payment of your choice: check, money order, or credit card.

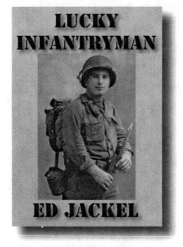

Lucky Infantryman by Ed Jackel

Ed Jackel spent just shy of two years serving in the United States Army during World War II. A young man older than most, he went on to do his duty when called. Mr. Jackel was one of many in the generation that truthfully saved the world and made it a much better place for those who would become his children and grandchildren.

In *Lucky Infantryman*, Eddie Jackel spins a wonderful story of great historical significance. This is an account every American should read. In the telling of his time in training for and in going to war, Ed Jackel does not glorify the events, does not politicize. He merely tells a soldier's story with all the genuineness and grit of growing up in America and being called on to do the seemingly impossible. To Eddie Jackel, and all the others who served, we say, "Thank you."

You may order online at www.bluewaterpress.com/lucky or by mail:

BluewaterPress LLC
52 Tuscan Way Ste 202-309
Saint Augustine FL 32092

Name: _____

Address: _____

City, State, Zip: _____

Phone number: _____

Email Address: _____

(All information kept in the strictest confidence)

Please send me Ed Jackel's *Lucky Infantryman*. Cost is $15.95 per copy. Shipping & handling is $3.95 per book for one copy, $6.95 for up to seven of any titles, and $1.15 per book for any combination of more than seven.

Number of books _____ x $15.95 = _____

Shipping and handling = _____

FL residents, please add sales tax for county of residence = _____

Total remitted = _____

We gladly accept payment of your choice: check, money order, or credit card.

Eagle Tales Edited by Joe Clark

This aviation anthology is a collection of flying stories written by the the faculty members of the Aeronautical Science Department of Embry-Riddle Aeronautical University, Daytona Beach campus. The professors teaching tomorrow's military and airline pilots were not always teachers; they too, spent time in the cockpits of various aircraft around the world, afloat on the high seas, and at flight levels.

If you are, were, want to be, or are planning to become a professional aviator, this is an enjoyable book that will give you insight into the life of working aviators. It's also a very enjoyable read.

A portion of each sale goes to the Jim Lewis Scholarship fund.

You may order online at www.bluewaterpress.com/eagletales or by mail:

BluewaterPress LLC
52 Tuscan Way Ste 202-309
Saint Augustine FL 32092

Name: _____

Address: _____

City, State, Zip: _____

Phone number: _____

Email Address: _____
(All information kept in the strictest confidence)

Please send me Joe Clark's *Eagle Tales*. Cost is $20.95 per copy. Shipping & handling is $3.95 per book for one copy, $6.95 for up to seven of any titles, and $1.15 per book for any combination of more than seven.

Number of books _____ x $20.95 = _____

Shipping and handling = _____

FL residents, please add sales tax for county of residence = _____

Total remitted = _____

We gladly accept payment of your choice: check, money order, or credit card.